The ABC's of Credit

Too Much Information –
Not Enough Time to Read the Small Print

Frances Anne Hernan
with
Faye Schliep
McGavick Field Publishing

Our sincerest appreciation to the Federal Trade Commission for their constant commitment to protect the American Consumer from fraudulent, deceptive and unfair business practices.

We would like to thank our project intern Elke Mermis for her professional contribution during the final stages of editing and proofing.

Cover Design: Quality Composition Service
Business Manager: Colleen Summers

Library of Congress Number: 2002116704

McGavick Field Publishing
Frances Anne Hernan
with Faye Schliep
118 N. Cherry
Olathe, KS 66061
The ABC's of Credit
Too Much Information - Not Enough Time to Read the Small Print

ISBN 0-9666928-3-7

Printed in the United States by Nationwide Printing, Olathe, Kansas.

The ABCs of Credit, Too Much Information – Not Enough Time to Read the Small Print, was written for and is dedicated to the American Consumer. Fifty percent of American households invest in the stock market. One hundred percent are consumers in the market place. Resources and recourses are provided for those individuals who cannot spend hundreds of hours on research to determine their rights.

Forward

I have long thought that my generation, "Generation X," would be better dubbed "Generation Excess." Those of us who have grown up in a world where anyone can get anything they want, at any time, have a tough time with certain concepts that should be second nature. Saving, waiting, or paying with cash are not activities with which we are very familiar.

My peers and I have been handed credit cards from the time we were teenagers. Yes, the creditors were given space to solicit in our college cafeterias. We were told getting credit cards would be the perfect way to "build good credit." We were not warned of the risks of paying with plastic now and not paying off the balance at the end of every month. There were no workshops on handling this very dangerous tool maturely; not an easy task at eighteen.

I ended up with three credit cards before the age of twenty, ran up $10,000 worth of debt, and worked on paying it off until I was thirty.

I wish I knew then what I know now.

I have learned my lessons and have spent a lot of time getting my finances in order. However, I still run into trouble that sometimes threatens to set me back. Recently I was surprised to find that a series of small charges on my bank card, that acts as both an ATM and credit card, had wracked up over $230 worth of insufficient funds charges on my account leaving my balance at negative $700! I was shocked and puzzled. After some research I found that my bank, which had recently been taken over by a larger bank, had now begun to allow charges even when there was no money in the account rather than decline transactions. As this was a new practice, I was unaware that my account had no money in it. I had never needed to keep track of exactly how much was in there because I knew that if there was no money, the transaction would be declined. I learned the hard way that that had changed.

Every kid entering college or going into the workforce should be required to read this book. Learning how to handle finances properly does not just happen as soon as you receive your first paycheck. It is something that is learned, through reading a book such as this or through the school of hard knocks.

If I knew then what I know now, I would have chosen to read this book, more than once, and take in all it has to offer.

The volume of information on fair credit practices available through the internet and in print form escapes most of us because we don't have the time to search for it, let alone understand the help that is available. This book pares the wealth of information down to the essentials.

A glossary and appendix in a book is often an afterthought. Not so in this book. Both the glossary and appendix are part of the body of the book. Much of this information is important for the well-being of your credit history. The forms in the appendix give you much needed insight into financial processes ahead of time. Learning the terms in the glossary will empower you with the knowledge you need whether you are shopping for better credit card interest rates or the lowest mortgage rates.

Whether you are just getting your finances back on track or have always been a good saver, you can learn from this book. There is something for everyone from credit reports to insurance policies to wills. Hernan knows that no one cares more about your money than you do. She makes us think. Think about the national economy and how it relates to each and every one of us. Instead of resisting taxes and social security from which we get some benefit, she implores us to avoid the high interest costs of credit card debt.

Fran Hernan has trodden the path of financial security for us. All we need to do is sit back and learn. And learn from her we can. Her experiences and savvy combine to make a wonderful concoction of a clear, concise reference that also makes a fun read. It is a far cry from many financial books that read like texts.

So sit back, have fun and get out your pen and paper and take notes. There will be a test later in the form of your financial well-being!

C. Halstead

Table of Contents

Introduction

Section One • Page 1
Closing the Gap
Take an inventory and develop your personal portfolio

Section Two • Page 15
Budget, Diet, Whatever
Counting and tracking is the key in both

Section Three • Page 23
How Important Is Your Credit Report?
*Is your credit report more important than
your birth certificate or marriage license?*

Section Four • Page 38
Points to Ponder
Using Credit wisely begins with choosing Credit Wisely.

Section Five • Page 54
Choosing a Lender and the Loan You Need
*Home equity loans, consolidating debt or
buying into certain foreclosure?*

Section Six • Page 60
Put Your Pride Aside
*When you run out of options, choose a debt management
program that can help you reduce your high interest debt.*

Section Seven • Page 67
Education Is The Key to Success.
College. . .but how to pay for it?

Section Eight• Page 82
In the Back of the Book
*An extended glossary of terms you will need across
the board in making financial decisions.*

Section Nine • Page 115
Appendix
*More small print and other information to
help you make the best choices as a consumer.*

Introduction

Economic Diversification:

As consumers many of us don't have a clue about the national economy that drives the market place and influences our everyday spending. Wall Street gets high on job cuts, then moans and groans when consumers don't spend enough to make their stock prices rise. In reality, essential spending for most of us depends on the employment we have. Unfortunately, unemployment often means loss of health care and other needs tied to everyday living.

Couples with a combined take-home income of $150,000 in the Midwest are doing very well. In New York or California, it's just a living. The homes and apartments in situation comedies like Friends or Everybody Loves Raymond sell (or rent) for much more than a dream house in the South or the Pacific Northwest.

According to the Ohio Self Sufficiency Standards a family including a parent, infant, pre-schooler and one school age child need an income of $2,182.60 a month, or $32,679.00 annually. The poverty threshold for this group is $16,333.00.

In 1994 in New York, the typical welfare recipient, a woman with two children, received a tax free benefit of $32,571. A tax payer would have to earn a salary of $45,000 to equal that amount.

On the other hand, in upstate New York, a single parent with two pre-school children needs a wage of $16.38 an hour to close the gap between basic needs for the family and income. Looking at national standards, gauging the median poverty level and the amounts needed for families to be self-sufficient, is a good way to compare what we think is a very good income compared with wage earners in other parts of the country.

Most of us never think about the poverty level, just as we don't think about living in mansions in Beverly Hills. It is important we develop our life style according to our personal standards and the local economy. At the same time we need to make an effort to understand the diversity of the national economy. A report on hourly wage standards to meet basic needs released by Californians for Family Economic Self Sufficiency states an adult with two children has to earn $25.55 an hour in Santa Clara County. Most of us have a hard time accepting this as an entry-level wage barely providing for basic needs. Check your own state numbers to see how you are faring.

Keep it Simple:

Organizing records will help you plan for the future and give you peace of mind. All bills and statements must be kept together each month, you shouldn't have to sift through tons of paper to figure out what is due when. There is hardly a day in our lives when we don't fight changes in schedules or have a mini crisis or two. The taste of victory when you win a dispute even for the cost of a book, or overcharges on a utility bill, is very sweet.

Give yourself time to examine your records over a six month or year period before you go start searching for the best mortgage. When looking to buy a home, arm yourself with as much information about property values, interest rates, closing costs and other fees. Bid wisely, don't submit a higher bid because a realtor mentions there is a lot of competition for the house. If you can't get a mortgage at a comfortable rate for the long term, and without compromising your total financial picture, let the dream house go. Wait a year or two when you have a larger down payment and are in a position to pay fewer points.

Check out your choice of credit cards and your bank. We operate in a free-market society and rates vary widely. There are a number of choices available to you – make your decisions wisely!

While you are concentrating on every day expenditures sometimes it is hard to think about setting long term goals. Most of us consider the three most important aspects of our long term plans to be, buying a home, paying for a college education for our children and planning for a secure retirement income.

Don't strictly prioritize saying when the mortgage is paid off, then we will start the college planning, and then saving for retirement. It doesn't work that way; you need to develop a perspective and plan for all three early on.

Closing the Gap

Many of us live day to day pretty confident we are taking care of our families and providing for all their needs including the future. The truth is we aren't always aware of what we need, and base our projections for the future on what we think we need.

It is very important to take a personal inventory, and develop a personal portfolio that includes all the things you have lined up for your protection. How much insurance do you have? If you have the attitude that life insurance and renter's insurance are not needed now, only some day, we want you to re-evaluate.

Your personal portfolio should be a collection of the savings, insurance and ownership papers you have. It should include your will and living will, arrangements for minor children in the event of your death if you are a single parent, or the death of both parents. Interim arrangements for the care of your children should be a part of this security papers collection.

We are not going to offer you charts and graphs written in percentages to impress upon you what you should have. I hate pie charts, and I hate percentages. If I have 100 dollars and spend 20, I have eighty dollars left, not 80 percent. Keeping records of your expenditures is one of the most important things you can do to stay on the road to a healthy financial existence.

Designating a file for important documents is one of the first steps you need to take to support the day to day record keeping of your expenditures and assets. Your personal papers will all have some financial value someday, even the living will and the arrangements for your children.

This value may become a negative when translated into the cost of facilitating your wishes. If you don't have a plan at work, if you never have written a will and you don't have arrangements for your children or even adult parents that live with you, thousands of dollars could be spent just trying to determine what you have, and how it should be distributed.

Developing a financial strategy for the future, to incorporate life style changes, including emergencies, is as important as paying the rent or the mortgage.

We don't want you to plan for disaster. But we do want you to be prepared for things that could change your life forever. It is difficult for young couples with a whole life ahead of them, to think about spending money on insurance, especially life insurance.

First order of business: Write a Will

We don't think about the importance of a will, because we don't feel we really have that much to will to anyone. Most mortgages have homeowners insurance, some with a pay off benefit if the bread winner dies before the mortgage is paid off.

There is a lot of talk today about prenuptial agreements, that protect one or both parties in the event of divorce or death. It is important for a couple to write a will as soon as they are married. Update your will every five years. You need to change your will when a major lifestyle event occurs, such as death or divorce. Wills are not that expensive. Write down all the things you want in the will. List your insurance policies and the beneficiaries and how you want property distributed.

It is a good idea to keep a copy of your living will, etc., with your homeowners insurance, life insurance, and custodial arrangements for your children in a safety deposit box.

Keep another copy of the will, living will etc., at home in a fire protected box or safe. Make a list of the numbers of the insurance policies, the company they are drawn on, the benefit amount and the beneficiaries. Make several copies of the list. Give the list to your executor, place a copy in your personnel file at work and your personal files. Give another copy to a family member.

Life Insurance Coverage

Before you let your fingers do the walking to search for an insurance agent, try to get a referral from co-workers and relatives. A word of caution. When an agent tries to avoid giving you information until you make a firm appointment, put him at the bottom of the list. Make it clear you are investigating other possibilities.

Insurance companies like most corporations spend millions of dollars advertising to underwrite your coverage. This is a big investment, and you need to take the time to read and evaluate all the possibilities.

We can not over emphasize the value of insurance protection. But remember insurance is sold on commission. As a consumer you have to determine what you need and decide what kind of policy you want, based on the coverage you can afford.

Don't approach purchasing life insurance with a pie in the sky attitude. Concentrate on providing a good living during your life time, not a great living after your death.

When determining the coverage you need for life insurance, factor in the ages of your children and the cost of living in your area. Life insurance is replacement income for your family. Start with a policy that can provide for minimum needs, and grow your insurance protection as you grow your income. It is important to start buying life insurance early because there may be conditions that arise in later years that affect your ability to get insurance and increase the premium.

When you decide on the coverage you want, answer all the questions honestly. Don't apply for a policy that offers lower premiums on certain conditions. Don't try to buy a non smoker's policy if you smoke two packs a day.

Never, Never, Never lie to an insurance company. To do so is jeopardizing your family and may be stripping them of the protection altogether.

Insurance companies may look at your credit report to determine your risk level. If you have public record information on your credit report that shows DWI's, it could increase your risk factor. Causing you to be refused outright, or be offered a policy with a much higher premium and less coverage that you applied for.

When you receive an adverse action notice (refusal to insure), request in writing as much information as possible. The adverse action notice will go into your credit report. Companies are required to remove this notice from your file in two years, make sure this is done.

Check out the benefits offered at your place of employment. If you are offered a life insurance policy as a part of your employment package, take it at the highest amount available. Ask the orientation facilitator if the policy remains in effect, if you leave their employment. Usually you can pick up the premium and continue the coverage.

Don't leave this to chance, make sure you understand all the benefits that are a part of the package, the exact terms and the potential for picking up the insurance in your name once you leave the company. Find out exactly what the value of your policy at work is and increase your insurance to meet the protection standard you have designed for your family.

In the final analysis, stick to your guns, buy the coverage you can afford. You are buying insurance for protection. It is important to project for the cost of this protection into living expenses and your safety cushion and figure it into your living expenses in the event of a life change, like unemployment, or serious illness. If you lose a policy because you can't afford the premium, you lose everything paid to date. Also it may be very difficult to get insurance, once you have lost it.

It is very important to have life insurance on every member of the family. If your spouse is a wage earner also, the insurance should be at the same level as yours, to give your family full protection.

A small policy on each child is very important. It may be hard for you to think about life insurance for a child, because the benefit is a death benefit. However, we don't know what the future holds, and the death of a child has enough emotional baggage you don't want to add to it by not being able to bury your loved one. This is an area you need to research and be very firm when purchasing this insurance. Buy a small policy and increase the value as the child grows.

If you are over forty and have never had insurance, you are going to find a lot of restrictions. One form of insurance you should consider seriously, is funeral insurance. You can buy as much funeral insurance as you want, depending on the arrangements you want.

Polices in the amount of 5,000 or 10,000 seem to be the best buy. It can be bought outright, or paid off in three, five or ten years.

Before you buy the policy and sign up for the shorter more expensive term, find out when the death benefit is available. If you are 60, don't be talked into the three year term if you can't afford it. The benefit will be paid if you die before the benefit is completely paid for, that is unless you lied in the application about your health.

When buying this coverage you have the opportunity to select the method of burial as well as the coffin, flowers and music. If you want to be cremated, it is wise to state this in the policy and more importantly in your will.

Health Insurance

Whatever your insurance is, you need to evaluate just how much coverage you have. What is the deductible? Define the coverage period, (June 1, 2002 to May 31, 2003). What are the restrictions?

When you get your policy, new or renewal, read it. This is one instance where reading the small print is very important. Compare the old policy to the new, see what changes are not mentioned in the legend. Enter the pertinent information in a check register that you keep just for that purpose, or at the front of your check register where we are supposed to record deposits. List the policy number, the provider, the coverage date and the deductible. When you write a check for a office visit, tests, or prescription medicine that have not met the deductible, highlight that in your check book.

At least once a month, add up all the medical bills you paid and transfer that total to the listing information on your check register. Keep the policy in a safe place but have the information you need at your fingertips.

You need to keep track of all those expenses the insurance company would not cover. If you are paying for your own insurance or contributing to your insurance at work you need this information to make an informed choice for coverage the next year.

Evaluate each years' expenditures and coverage against the expenses not covered. This evaluation will reveal whether or not you have enough coverage. If you don't have enough coverage, it might be time to consider supplemental insurance. Check first with your company to see if supplemental insurance is offered through the company. Make this a priority. Supplemental policies can be very expensive, but it is one instance when more is more. Paying more now makes more sense than trying to pay for uncovered expenses later.

Catastrophic illnesses or injuries from accidents can destroy a family, particularly if that injury or illness affects a child or the bread winner.

No matter how secure you feel about your employment and your medical insurance, you have to be cognizant of the possibility that unemployment can mean the end of your insurance, with very little notice. You don't want to think about it constantly but you have to be aware of it. It can happen to you.

Instead we are suggesting that you need to evaluate your monthly living expenses from cable service to your utility bills. If you have premium cable and enjoy it and use it to near max; you don't have to chuck it to save money. On the other hand if you have every channel known to man, and you watch it less than four hours a week, reconsider.

The same goes with your internet service. Do you really need to surf to the end of the internet in the fastest time possible? If your computer system is part of a home business or network to your employment, you may need the best and the fastest.

However if you spend less than 10 hours a week on the internet, you aren't saving that much time. Are you getting what you are paying for? I spend several hours a day on the internet doing research for various life projects, communicating with friends, and playing games to unwind. The dial up service I have serves my need. When I contact the Internet Service Provider (ISP) with a question or problem, I get a response within 24 hours. That is a much shorter turn around time than most consumer services. My service is provided through my local telephone company. I don't have to worry about missing a payment, because the payment is made through the bill.

If you really want the fastest service available investigate the monthly cost, along with the installation. About a year ago a neighbor told me she was getting DSL service with the same phone company that I had the dial up service. She said she had ordered the kit, but her son had not had time to install it. She was paying for the unit, and the service and had never installed it. She asked me if I would look at it. I did, just long enough to read in the instructions on how easy it was to assemble, with the disclaimer if you need expert advice our technicians will install it for $200.00.

A salesperson convinced her she needed this service since she knew very little about the internet. I told the same company I was computer literate, they sold me the dialup service. It took several phone calls to get my friend's service disconnected and several months to get the unit charges removed from her bill.

Before you sign any contract for an ISP, long distance service, cable service, or cell phone contracts, read the small print. It is usually buried in all the promises. Don't sign a contract you don't fully understand. Don't sign up for a service that isn't on a month to month basis unless you understand all the secrets of the deal. If you decide you don't want a service because you are not getting enough use out of it, or it is too expensive for your needs, you may not be able to drop it if you signed a contract. Sometimes you can get a reduced fee by buying into a contract, don't do it.

Read, read and read again:

You really need to evaluate every section of that cell phone contract. If the salesmen implies you can get special coverage, get it in writing. The communication industry is very competitive. A better deal may be just around the corner. Don't be locked into contracts that are very costly. Read the small print not only about the time you are signing up for but the services provided.

No matter how many minutes you have, it's the day time minutes that count and disappear quickly. A friend told me recently that she had to make a couple of long distance calls before nine P.M. She assumed that the night time minutes would kick in at nine. Instead the calls were charged at the full day time rate because they started before nine. She looked at her contract and there it was. She paid the bill, but she warned everyone she knew.

Don't fall prey to a phone service offer that seems too good to be true. The competitiveness of the communications industry has created a bombardment of offers for low rate service like the pre-approved credit cards. Again, the selling points are in bold print, the true aspects of the contract in tiny print you can't read.

Everyone wants your long distance service because cell phones are really cutting into their profits. If the new service sounds interesting, check with your current service to see just how many changes you can make to bring your phone bill in line with your needs and the newest offer. Before you consider any offer, look at your current phone bill. Do you need every service you are being billed for?

I just had to have caller ID; I got rid of it when I realized that 75% of the callers were not identified. My phone unit has an answering machine. However, I have call-waiting because I spend a good deal of time on the computer. The only thing that will increase the efficiency of call waiting, is for me to learn to check for messages when I am off the computer.

Check each item on your bill. If you have a cell phone, do you need the lowest rate possible, (with a fee) for long distance? If you have a computer line, use that line to make calls to keep the other line free. Give the number to family members.

If you decide to switch either your long distance service, or your full service make sure you understand exactly what you are getting. Recently a friend of mine tried a new service, her first bill was full of hidden charges and extras.

Leasing Personal Automobiles

Moving up to a luxury class car, a recreational vehicle or getting that a nifty little sports car may have a lot more hidden costs and conditions than you can afford when it is time to turn the car back to the dealer. Making a big payment, sometimes thousands of dollars just to get in the car, will not go toward depreciation or other factors when turn in time comes. The buy back or turn in charge can be much higher than you anticipated because you have not taken as good of care of the vehicle as the dealer demands.

Get the agreement, and study it, don't just skim it. Circle items you have questions about. Before you sign make sure you understand every single line item. Ask questions. Pay attention to phrases like, "if such and such happens although it probably won't, you are responsible". Negotiate to change anything not acceptable, and to get the best lease deal.

Before you go through with any leasing program, check out the price of purchasing the same car. Will the trade in allowance you would get equal the outlay of the down payment for the lease? How much higher or lower will lease payments be than purchase payments? If there is not a big enough difference, why lease?

About Retirement; don't wait until tomorrow to plan.

Along the road to retirement you should pick up several possibilities for income, from pensions, 401 K's, IRA's, bonds, even inheritances. It is important that you know what you have now and what you will have five, ten, fifteen even 20 years from now. It is just as important to check your benefits and savings totals as it is to compare you expenditures and coverage for health insurance. You might get dizzy if you do an in depth check every month, but you should do a quick check each quarter and when tax time comes do an annual review of your retirement funds. Pay attention to what is going on in the world around you. If you have a pension from a previous employer that is involved in a merger or take over, don't wait until you get a notification in the mail regarding your benefits, check it out.

Knowing how much to put where might not be an easy decision. Many decisions will depend on the time you start in earnest to develop a plan. If you want to convert different plans into a major plan, don't do it on your own. We are not suggesting you that you spend a small fortune to learn how to save money. Every option will have a fee or charge from mutual funds to stocks. The other side of the coin is you need to understand not only the savings you can accrue but also the taxes on interest and investments. List what you have now, and the areas you think you would like to explore. Your attorney or a Certified Public Accountant is a good place to start. If they can't advise you they may be able to make a referral that will meet your financial needs with less risk than picking a financial planner out of the yellow pages. It is very important to understand the tax consequences, along with the fees and other charges of every aspect of your investments.

The cry of each generation is: "will it be there when we retire"? In fact in recent years there has been a lot of buzz about the possible privatization of Social Security. Many of us have no idea what privatization means let alone understand how it will affect us. While it is still in the talking stage, not much above campaign rhetoric, like the Social Security lock box, you have to investigate the facts and determine how it involves your personal payroll taxes.

A good place to start is understanding the program and just how much we pay into the program. Between your contribution and the employer match you may not have enough income to live comfortably. Do you know how much of our income goes into this payroll tax? The answer might surprise you. The cap for contributions is $82,500 (2002). An even bigger surprise is your max contribution (7.65%) is $6,311.50. With the employer match the total contribution to the entitlement is $12,622.00. If your gross income is $40,000 a year, with your contribution and the employer match the maximum contribution to your account is $6,120.00 for that tax year. While we can't figure out or have access to how your entitlement will be computed we do know that 15% of our current income is not going to get us very far if that is the only plan we have. Most of us gripe about the Social Security deduction but we don't really know much about the program. Do you wonder if you will ever get a return on your contribution?

When will you retire, at 62 or 65? New Social Security eligibility rules have extended the retirement date beginning this year. If you are going to have little other income in terms of pensions and investments you need to start thinking now about other options available to you. Can you enter retirement with your house paid off, a late model car, and good health insurance? This doesn't happen overnight.

Medicare is not a coverall. Supplemental insurance is a must not only to cover office visits, medical procedures and prescriptions but emergency transportation. We don't have a crystal ball. Not only do you have to know just what your assets are you need to learn how to do everything you can to protect them. Nursing home insurance should seriously be considered because of the possibility that one spouse could need very expensive long term care, while the other spouse will fight to survive financially on what is left of their estate after all medical bills are paid. Life insurance is an asset you can borrow on, just as is the equity in your home if you need to provide for emergency situations. However, you don't want this to disappear. Here is one area where a consultant can help you prepare for situations that could otherwise destroy you both financially and emotionally.

We live in a different work environment than the generations before us that worked maybe two or three jobs in their entire life. Now we often move up financially by changing companies. Or we make a lateral move that involves more benefits and opportunities to move up the ladder. Health insurance, life insurance, pensions and investment plans often play a major role in the process when we seek employment.

Each time you make an employment decision you need to carefully consider what the long term affects will be on your retirement. Can you roll over the benefits from one employer to another? If you worked for a state government with a private system for Social Security like the one offered in Ohio, think twice before you cash out the benefit. Don't let the idea of the money burn a hole in your pocket. If you keep the money invested in the program, when you are ready to retire, the amount you get annually might bridge the gap between Social Security and other pension income. If you do cash out make sure you know when the buy back period ends should you decide that you took the wrong option.

Even though you can't get your benefits now, it is your money and whether it is your Social Security benefit, pensions, investments and other savings you have to keep track of the growth of each fund and make adjustments for any losses that occur.

If you look at Social Security as a pot of gold at the end of the rainbow providing your income after retirement, you need a reality check.

We haven't offered a lot of numbers here. The economy is so diversified it would be impossible for us to come up with a standard.

Also, we don't identify or recommend a company by name. The purpose of this book is to alert the consumer to protections available to them. We have no interest in selling insurance, cell phones, or automobiles.

Social Security Retirement Planner

Social Security Full Retirement and Reductions by Age

No matter what your full retirement age
(also called "normal retirement age") is,
you may start receiving benefits as early as age 62

Year of Birth	Full Retirement Age	Age 62 Reduction Months	Monthly % Reduction	Total % Reduction
1937 or earlier	65	36	.555	20.00
1938	65 and 2 months	38	.548	20.83
1939	65 and 4 months	40	.541	21.67
1940	65 and 6 months	42	.535	22.50
1941	65 and 8 months	44	.530	23.33
1942	65 and 1 0 months	46	.525	24.17
1943-1954	66	48	.520	25.00
1955	66 and 2 months	50	.516	25.84
1956	66 and 4 months	52	.512	26.66
1957	66 and 6 months	54	.509	27.50
1958	66 and 8 months	56	.505	28.33
1959	66 and 10 months	58	.502	29.17
1960 and later	67	60	.500	30.00

You can also retire at any time between age 62 and full retirement age. However, if you start at one of these early ages, your benefits are reduced a fraction of a percent for each month before your full retirement age.

As a general rule, early retirement will give you about the same total Social Security benefits over your lifetime, but in smaller amounts to take into account the longer period you will receive them.

Here's An Important Point: There are disadvantages and advantages to taking your benefit before your full retirement age. The advantage is that you collect benefits for a longer period of time. The disadvantage is that your benefit is permanently reduced. Each person's situation is different, so make sure you contact Social Security before you decide to retire.

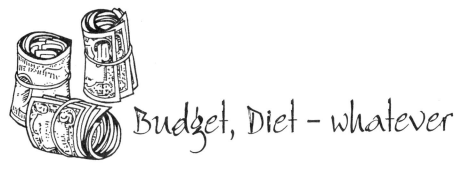

Budget, Diet – whatever

Diets and budgets are both important in our lives as they keep us focused on the long-term goal whether it is physical or fiscal.

How many programs have you joined where you have paid good money for bad food and likewise spent money on budget busting items that you later discover you really didn't need.

When determining your expenses and designing a plan it really isn't that different from designing a diet to lose weight. We need to keep our eye on all the numbers, not just the calories or the daily bank balance. The numbers that are important in dieting are your cholesterol and blood pressure, in budgeting pay attention to monthly expenses and interest rates.

No matter how diligently you plan, something always happens to throw your finances a curve. Usually little things with a big price tag. The month with the biggest obligations, insurance payment due, and large heating bill, is when the washer breaks and the car needs repairs.

Looking back on the last year, how many costly surprises did you have? Did you have the resources to deal with the emergencies? Or did you have to spend right up to the limit on a credit card you just got down to a reasonable amount?

Develop a seven year plan:

Instead of chasing unrealistic goals for 30 or 40 years, consider a shorter, easier to manage period like seven years. We are advised to hold on to major receipts and contracts for seven years. It takes seven years to erase bad credit on your credit report.

Rethink your priorities each time you design a new seven year plan. Your priorities will change as your lifestyle needs change. The first plan may reflect high childcare costs and the commitment to buy a home. Your needs and your resources will determine how you design your plan.

Corporations project earnings and profits on a quarterly basis. If you are self employed or live off of your investment income, you file estimated taxes, quarterly.

Developing a financial strategy, and projecting your needs on a quarterly instead of an annual basis will provide better records. It will be a lot easier to deal with a quarter, 13 weeks, than to project a whole year of needs and expenditures. Using a seven-year model and quarterly accounting will produce records that won't enslave or mislead you.

You don't need a shoebox of receipts.

The accounting starts with your check register and bank statement. The accountability starts with evaluating and reviewing your fixed expenses. Divide your cancelled checks into categories. Start with housing, utilities, loans(car), and insurance. Continue the list with the other monthly expenses: phone, cable, internet etc. At the bottom list your credit cards, whether bank cards or department store credit.

First step is to get your tax records and bank statements for the previous year. Use these documents to set up projections for next quarter. Your check register and statement reflect some of the unexpected expenditures of the past year. How much of that expense was transferred to credit cards? Can you figure out at a glance how much you were spending on the basic needs? Probably not. Instead try to track the past year's expenses through events. Like the birth of a child, the purchase of a new home, a child starting pre school or college. Have you had any major illnesses or a job loss in the last seven years? Did you have to cash out bonds or CDs? How many times have you started a savings account, only to withdraw the money to pay for an emergency?

Interest on automobile loans and mortgages are part of the bargain to provide for your needs. High interest on credit cards, for needs or wants is costing you on average of twenty dollars out of every one hundred dollars. The interest becomes the controlling influence on your finances. The recycled high interest credit card debt can be just as costly to your mental health and finances as the pound gain is to your physical health.

Add up the expenses for each month separately. Add those totals together, then divide by three. Most likely there will be a gap and the totals won't match the actual monthly totals. This is why doing a quarterly projection makes sense. In the middle month you might have a heating bill for over 250 dollars because of sub zero temperatures. When that payment is due the same time your Christmas purchases kick in on your credit cards, the payments will clash.

What are your top three financial objectives?

Prioritize. Decide early, which of the many possible financial goals are really worth pursuing and start working toward them. Keep in mind: Both long and short-term goals will take a hit from time to time. Keeping spending within your income is not going to be possible day in and day out. Develop a strategy that gives you confidence to use credit wisely. Learn to recognize the periods that impact your ability to meet expenses. You need to find a way to grow your assets and reduce high interest credit.

Creating a plan:

Creating a budget involves three basic steps: Identifying, evaluating and tracking.

Government figures show that many households are spending more than they bring in, regardless of their income level. If you fall in this category, you do need to take stock of where you are headed.

If you don't have software to design a worksheet that suits your needs, use a yellow legal pad to record figures. Starting with your check list, create a budget with pen and paper. If you have a software program that you are comfortable with, you can transfer the figures to the accounting information on the computer. You will do more figuring but the process of transferring to a spread-sheet might be the thing that helps you imprint the figures in your mind. Your check register is a good place to start as you develop categories.

Use a simple formula, give your spouse the utilities, car pay-ment, repair bills etc., and you take the rest. Even with the kitchen table approach we understand that trying to keep track of expenses and budgeting is not the best togetherness activity. This way you can create a little competition instead of friction. Trade off the responsibilities every quarter.

Fall back on a safety cushion:

One of the first aspects of your personal financial goal should be to create a fall back plan for emergencies.

Start saving for the future by building a safety cushion for emergencies that result from life changes you have no control over. The amount you need depends on your income and your day to day family expenses. If your monthly income is $2,000, your goal should be 3 times that or $6,000. To reach this goal, start today and save something from each payday. The amount you start with isn't as important as getting into the habit, and setting a goal. Put away one-hour's wages a week (for each wage earner), or the highest amount of interest on one of your monthly credit cards.

When unplanned events occur, (i.e. job loss, sickness, or death) you will have financial support in your most vulnerable emotional times.

As soon as you reach the minimum amount your bank accepts for deposit for CDs, transfer the money from your passbook account. Put the money in the bank, not a piggy bank, or envelope. It is a lot harder to get at during times of stress than if you have it sitting around. You want to be able to get to your safety cushion without penalty if you need it. Concentrate on short-term savings before you develop long term investments.

Keep it simple

One of the reasons we lose control of budgets on paper is we don't have time to spend tracking and listing every penny. Your bank statement, your pay stubs and monthly bills show most of your expenditures for each quarter. A bank statement from the last quarter can help project expenses for the next quarter. Rely on your own common sense and your records.

Your mortgage payment includes homeowners insurance, taxes and interest. In the future, when figuring your rent payment, add 10%. That ten percent should be earmarked for increases in the rent and your next move. If you save 10% of your rent for three years (45.00/450), when you start looking for a bigger or better place you will have a head start without stripping your checking account for down payments.

Using Credit Wisely

It is wise to budget your credit in such a way that you have it available for large insurance payments to give you more monthly cash flow. You pay that insurance off in three months on the card, before you get the next premium. Making the big payment on a credit card you know you will pay off in time to make the next payment is much smarter than using your credit card to pay for the shortages caused by the big payment.

If your monthly expenditures for three months exceed your income, you need to readjust. This is where you need to determine needs from wants. Building debt to cover wants could land you in a position that prevents you from ever reaching your long-term goals.

One of the worst habits you can develop is using credit, (cash advances and convenience checks) to pay for standard on going expenses. The interest you will pay on an unpaid utility or phone bill is much lower than what you pay on a cash advance.

When you buy a big item on credit remember, you are not only paying interest on the cost of the purchase, but you are paying interest on the sales tax. On an item over a thousand dollars that is considerable.

Late fees, overdraft charges and over the limit fees.

Late fees on a credit card account and overdraft charges on your checking account are very costly. This could be just procrastination, but you need to make sure those payments are in on time. Take advantage of electronic bill pay offered by most banks. You can schedule the payments automatically or enter each payment according to your pay schedule and the due date. If you have overdraft protection on your checking account, or if you can transfer money from savings or another account into your checking account, you can deal with surprises and unexpected problems with much less difficulty.

Electronic withdrawals or debit card transactions also give you a transaction list on your statement that will help determine where and how you are disbursing funds.

Your bank statement provides a wealth of information regarding monthly expenditures, transactions, and mistakes. Both yours and the banks. Banks and credit card companies are obligated to correct mistakes. The catch is, it is your responsibility to provide the information to correct the error. You have to do this in a timely manner. When you find an error on a credit card or bank statement when getting ready for your taxes in April that occurred in August of the previous year, you may be out of luck. Credit card companies give you very little time to bring the error to their attention and to dispute it.

Itemize your reserves:

Your checking account, and your savings, (including money market accounts, CDs and bonds) are reserves. Your checking account is going to be your main resource for living expenses.

If you have developed bad habits over the years in keeping an up to date and accurate check register, this is your first order of business. Take the time to enter every check you write. At the end of the day, transfer the amount and date to your register. The date and amount is really all you need in a register if you have duplicate checks and it will give you the information to reconcile your statement without flipping through the check book.

Savings are important. Set a comfortable standard for saving that you can meet. Long-term savings are great for college, retirement etc., once you have reached your emergency cushion goal. Build the long-term increments related to the needs of the short term.

Don't be blinded by the advantages of compound interest on savings. Time is on your side when saving, it is your enemy when compiling interest on debt. One of the drawbacks of monitoring on paper is the totals sometimes look too good. Don't create a paper trail that is difficult to keep up with. If you need more than two legal size sheets to reconcile your monthly expenses, you are even in bigger trouble than most of us.

Keep track of your ATM withdrawals on a weekly basis. Set a limit and a day to use the ATM for spending cash, either on Monday, or the weekend, not both days. You cannot control your expenditures if you are not cognizant of your spending habits. Calculate what you are spending as cash, and if it is over 8%, it's too much.

Beware of "spending creep", as your annual income climbs from raises and or promotions don't change your spending habits immediately. If you get a substantial raise figure out how much will go for taxes. This would be a good time to add to your emergency fund, before you start spending the increase on incidentals. If the raise is not designated to playing catch up because of poor management or a life event, wait six months to incorporate the raise into your spending plan.

If one of the wage earners is in the National Guard, don't figure this into your income. In the event a reservist is called up, the gap between active duty pay and professional income can be staggering for the lower ranks. Companies have to hold your job, they don't have to pay your rent. Put your income from the reservist paycheck into a savings account and convert it to a CD once a year. A member of the National Guard or Reserves does have some relief available if called to active duty in situations like Desert Storm or 9-11. Be sure to check this out.

Re-evaluate your IRS deductions.

If you are getting more than a thousand dollars back each year you should look at rearranging your deductions. The money you are allowing the government to use could pay a winter utility bill. Money you get back at the end of the tax year in your refund, is your money. Instead of lending the government money at no interest, add that to your savings for your safety cushion. Figure what you owe for this year; take the deductions that won't interfere with your obligation for next year. Your total tax bill will not be any different and you will have a little more income. If you do get that refund, make an extra mortgage payment or use it towards a down payment on a car.

Even if you are in a credit situation where you benefit from lower interest on car payments and mortgages you still need to consider making bigger and even extra payments to get the maximum savings on your interest. Especially on your mortgage. Using our seven-year theme for your finances, re-evaluate your mortgage and interest for refinancing purposes at least once during each cycle.

Beware of luxuries dressed as necessities.

If your income doesn't cover your expenses, you need to balance needs with wants.

When setting priorities, narrow your objectives. You probably won't be able to achieve every financial goal you have ever dreamed of. Focus first on the goals that matter (your living expenses encompass most of them, housing, shelter, food, insurance). Identify your primary expenses and categorize your primary goals based on what you are spending with more emphasis on the short-term future than the long term.

Be prepared for conflicts with goals competing with each other. When faced with such a conflict, choose by applying criteria that will benefit family members in the long run. In drawing up your list of goals and expenses you should look for things that will help you feel financially secure. Once you have your list together, you need to rank the items in order of importance and place them on your 7-year grid. The fact is many of us live day to day never thinking about expenditures or the future past the next pay check.

Goal Setting Worksheet

Express your goals as positive statements, and be specific and realistic. Place your most important goals at the top of your list.

Short-Term Goals

_____

_____

_____

_____

_____

Medium-Term Goals

_____

_____

_____

_____

_____

Long-Term Goals

_____

_____

_____

_____

How Important is Your Credit Report?

The Federal Trade Commission (FTC) works for the consumer to prevent fraudulent, deceptive and unfair business practices in the marketplace and to provide information to help consumers spot, stop and avoid them.

The Fair Credit Reporting Act provides services and guidance to the consumer by defining the responsibilities and liabilities of businesses that provide information to and access data from the Credit Reporting Agencies (CRA). The Fair Credit Reporting Act (FCRA) is designed to promote accuracy, fairness, and privacy of information in the files of every consumer-reporting agency. Every single credit situation, transaction and reporting mechanism is covered in this act. It is the best piece of legislation for protecting consumers.

The problem is many of us are so bogged down with acronyms we don't understand and may miss the true value of this agency. It is truly big brother in every good sense of the term. If the wrong information or outdated information is on your report, it can have almost as negative an impact as a criminal record.

Although you are notified in writing when a company orders such a report, and you can request certain information about the report, the CRA does not have to reveal the sources of the information. This sounds like the Privacy of Information turned inside out.

Inaccurate information must be corrected or deleted. A credit-reporting agency must remove or correct inaccurate or unverified information from your files, usually within 30 days after you dispute it. In addition, the CRA must give you a written notice telling you it has corrected or removed the disputed information. As we stated in the budget section, it is very important for you to know what is in your report. Although the report shouldn't change much from year to year, there is always the possibility a mistake could prove very costly.

Credit Reporting Agencies:

Credit bureaus gather and sell information about you, (such as if you pay bills on time or filed bankruptcy), to creditors, employers, landlords, and other businesses. You can find the complete text of the Fair Credit Report Act online at http://www.ftc.gov/. You may contact a state or local consumer protection agency or state attorney to learn your rights regarding credit history reporting and other consumer issues that could impact you and your history.

You must be told when your file has been used against you, resulting in a denial of an application for credit, insurance or employment by the CRA that provided the consumer report.

You can find out what is in your file. The CRA must give you the information in your file and a list of everyone who has requested it recently. There is no charge for the report if a person has taken action against you because of information supplied by the credit bureau. You must request the report within 60 days of receiving notice of the action. You are also entitled to one free report every twelve months upon request if you certify that you are unemployed and plan to seek employment within 60 days, that you are on welfare, or your report is inaccurate due to fraud. Otherwise, a CRA can charge up to eight dollars for a report.

Although we all have had dealings with a credit bureau at one time or another, I doubt that few of us understand the power and the scope of the CRA.

Also few of us understand our rights, or how to assert those rights. We don't fully understand how a report with erroneous information can impact our ability to obtain credit or even rent a house or apartment.

One of the most frightening aspects of Credit Reporting Agencies is they can create detailed reports that involve interviews with your neighbors, co workers or acquaintances. These reports can be ordered by an insurance company or a prospective employer. These reports seem to mimic the investigations the military do to secure information about a soldier for a top security clearance. Right after I joined my husband in Morocco in 1960, two men were questioning my neighbors about my parents. When they questioned one neighbor the man got very upset, chased the two men off his porch and went in and called the police. The dispatcher knew my father well; he was from our neighborhood. He sent a patrol car out and the two men turned out to be representatives from the Defense Intelligence Service. These officers were investigating my background because of my husband's security clearance

Actions and notations on your credit report:

Your account condition is the data that shows the status of the account, current, past due, charged off, closed, or too new to rate. Accounts in good standing are those accounts that are positive with no delinquencies and go into determining your risk level.

Your credit report includes the creditor's name and address, the status of the account, amount owed and credit line. Important factors in the report are not only the payment history, but how many accounts you have, and how close to the limit the accounts are.

Most items on your report will not stay more than seven years. However the status of account will reflect the last ninety days of non-payment and whether or not the account was charged off. If you had a good payment history for four years, then a life event ruined your ability to pay, the account won't reflect the good years. This is unfortunate down the line because you will only be judged by that bad period. When and if you are able to get credit again, surely some of the past history will prevail, at least five years into your credit report future. In other words if you started having problems in 2000 that will be reflected in your history until 2007. The good payment record will have long been discarded.

When you sign a credit or employment application you give the prospective creditor or employer the right to secure your credit report. You also give the creditor the right to monitor your report. This scanning of your account helps the creditor to gain information to help them manage their financial risk. Accounts in good standing help establish your credit worthiness and may determine credit line increases.

Reports contain information that lead to creditors developing scores based on the risk factor of the accounts in your credit history. Your credit score is determined by placing you in a risk category that compares you to a large number of consumers with a similar credit behavior.

Factors that determine your score include your total debt, types of accounts, number of late payments, and the length of time the accounts have been open. Because risk score models are developed to predict your future payment ability, your account status that leads to the score could have a positive or negative result.

Commonly Asked Questions About Credit Files

Q: Why did you turn down my request for credit?
A: Credit reporting agencies do not recommend that your credit application be accepted or rejected. Credit grantors make that decision based on your payment record and their own criteria.

Q: Do credit reporting agencies rate my accounts?
A: No. All we do is maintain records. Each creditor reports the status of your account according to your manner of payment.

Q: How can I correct a mistake in my credit files?
A: complete the Research Request form and give details of the information you believe is incorrect. We will then check with the credit grantor, collection agency or public record source to see if any error has been reported. Information that cannot be verified will be removed from your file. If you and a credit grantor disagree on any information, you will need to resolve the dispute directly with the credit grantor who is the source of the information in question.

Q: What is in my credit file that keeps me from attaining credit?
A: We do not know, since credit reporting agencies do not grant credit. Each credit grantor has established criteria for making credit decisions. Your credit may appear to be perfect, but having too much credit or too many outstanding balances are examples of why your request for credit might be declined. Sometimes the decision is not even based directly on the credit file; for instance, you may not have been at your current residence or in your present job long enough. If you have any questions about why you were not approved for credit, contact the credit grantor who turned you down for credit for an explanation.

Q: Why is my last reported employment outdated?
A: What is listed as your last reported employment is actually the last employment reported by credit grantors. Employment information is typically reported from applications for credit and therefore is not regularly updated. This information is not used by credit grantors or employers in making their decision, but is used for demographic purposes.

Q: Is the credit score part of my credit file?
A: *The credit score is not a part of your credit file. It is a process that assists the credit grantor during the credit application process. The score may change as your credit information changes.*

Q: If I do have credit problems, is there some place where I can get advice and assistance?
A: *Yes, there are several organizations that offer assistance. For example, the Consumer Credit Counseling Service (CCCS) is a non-profit organization that offers free or low-cost financial counseling to help solve their financial problems. CCCS can help you analyze your situation and work with you to develop solutions. There are more than 600 CCCS offices throughout the country. Call 1-800-388-2227 for the telephone number of the office nearest you.*

Q: Should I use one of those companies that promise to help "fix" my credit?
A: *That is your choice. Remember, however, that these companies cannot have accurate information removed from your credit file. Much of what they do you can do for yourself at little or no cost.*

What is a credit score?

A credit score is a composite that indicates how likely you are to pay on a loan or credit card as agreed. It is a predictor of performance. It is one piece of information credit grantors use when evaluating your application for credit. Your credit score may be based solely on information in your credit files with the credit reporting agencies. Other scores may be based on a combination of credit information and other information you supply on your credit application.

The way you have handled credit in the past may have a link as to how you will manage credit in the future.

Credit scores cannot predict with certainty how you or anyone will manage credit. They do provide an objective estimate of how likely you are to repay on time and according to terms.

The credit score is not a part of your credit file. It is a process that assists the credit grantor during the credit application process. The score will change as your credit information changes.

Remember there is a big difference between organizations that offer assistance to help you solve your financial problems, analyze your situation and work with you to develop solutions and the companies that promise to fix your credit. Point scoring is the assignment of values for characteristics identified as indicators of a person's credit worthiness and used in developing the score models that will determine your ability to pay and reflect your credit risk level.

High-risk consumers may only be able to get credit with very high interest rates. This consumer will have a great deal of difficulty buying a home because of bankruptcies, chargeoffs, delinquencies and or public record items on their report.

Score factors are elements from your credit report that drive your credit score. Statistical models are used to generate credit scores. Your information is analyzed against millions of other consumer credit reports to identify and determine future creditworthiness in the form of a credit score.

Adverse Action Notice

When you are refused insurance or denied increased coverage and that decision is based on your credit report, the FCRA requires the insurance company to provide a notice of adverse action. The notice must include the name of the Credit Reporting Agency that supplied the information.

Notice:

Upon receipt of your dispute, we first review and consider the relevant information you have submitted regarding the nature of your dispute. If that review does not resolve your dispute and further investigation is required, we provide notification of your dispute, including the relevant information you submitted, to the source that furnished the dispute information to us. The source reviews the information we provided, conducts an investigation with respect to the disputed information, and reports the results back to us. We then make deletions or changes to your credit file as appropriate based on the results on the reinvestigation. The name and address and, if reasonably available, the phone number of the furnisher(s) of information we contacted while processing your dispute(s) is shown under the Results of Your Investigation section on the cover letter that accompanies the copy of your revised credit file.

If you still disagree with an item after it has been verified, you may send to us a brief statement, not to exceed 100 words (200 words for residents of the state of Maine), explaining the nature of your disagreement. Your statement will become part of your credit file and will be disclosed each time your credit file is accessed.

If the reinvestigation results in a change to or deletion of the information you are concerned about, or you submit a statement in accordance with the preceding paragraph, you have the right to request that we send your revised credit file to any company that received your credit file in the past six months for any purpose (12 months for Colorado, New York, New Jersey and Maryland residents) or in the past two years for employment purposes.

1026311R-5-98 USA

Even when the information was not the final criteria for the denial of insurance or a rate increase on a current policy, the disclosure of it is important. A Credit Reporting Agency is not responsible for the decision in insurance requests just as they are not responsible when credit is denied. The CRA reports the information supplied on a monthly basis by your creditors.

Also, disclosure of this information is very important because some consumer reports contain errors. If there is an error the consumer has the right to dispute the accuracy and completeness of the information that caused the denial of credit or insurance.

You must request a copy of the report within 60 days. The CRA has no knowledge or interest in the decisions made as they supply the information only. You have an obligation to ferret out the reasons for the denial as soon as possible if you plan to supply the insurance company with information you dispute on your report.

Right to dispute inaccurate information:
You have the right to inform the CRA when you discover your file contains inaccurate information. Inaccurate information must be corrected or deleted.

A credit-reporting agency must remove or correct inaccurate or unverified information from its files, usually within 30 days after you dispute it. In addition the CRA must give you a written notice telling you of their corrections and other actions.

The CRA must investigate the items usually within 30 days by presenting to its information source all relevant evidence you submit, unless your dispute is frivolous. The source must review your evidence and report its findings to the CRA. The source must also advise national credit report agencies to which it has provided the data of any error. The CRA must give you a written report of the investigation (credit repair) and a copy of your report if the investigation results in any change. If the CRA does not resolve the dispute, you may add a brief statement to your file. The CRA must normally include a summary of your statement in future reports. If an item is deleted or a disputed statement is filed, you may ask that anyone who has recently received your report be notified of the change.

The FTC through the FCRA affords the consumer protection from credit card companies in many ways. However the late fees, over the limit fees and charges for non-sufficient checks, are way out of line and there is no cap on these charges. You have the responsibility to choose a company with fair and reasonable rates. When you pay your bill on time and stay within limits, these costs are not an issue.

One of the consumers we interviewed stated she had a stroke and was hospitalized and then put in a rehabilitation center (nursing home) for four weeks. She was very lucky with the physical aspects but she nearly had another stroke when she got home and started opening her mail. This woman had several little charge accounts (balances low but limit also low.) She missed two payments. Her monthly payment was $20.00, which she paid every month. Her balance on the account was $120.00; her credit limit was $200.00. She missed two payments. She was charged a late fee and interest which took the balance to $160.00. She missed the second payment and was charged another late fee of $35.00 and an over the limit fee of $35.00. Only after a letter from her doctor was the matter resolved. They removed all the charges. It took six months to do this. Most of us don't know what to do, and if we did, we aren't always certain the time involvement is worth it. It is.

Public Record information:

A CRA can report criminal convictions, this makes the credit report important for prospective employers. Whether it is due to the Privacy of Information act of 1974 or Human Resource restrictions imposed by the federal government, there is very little an employer can ask about a prospective hire. A past employer can only give a reference as to whether or not they will rehire a former employee. Discharge information can not be reported unless the employee was prosecuted for a crime against the employer and it is part of public record.

The public record section details liens including bankruptcies citing class, state or origin and release date. Most of us don't look at our credit report as a history of every corner of our lives; maybe we should.

SAMPLE CREDIT FILE

Personal Identification Information

Your Name
123 Current Address
City, State 00000

Social Security #:   123-45-6789
Date of Birth: April 10th, 1940

Previous Address(es)
456 Former Rd. Atlanta, GA 30000
P.O. Box XXXX Savannah, GA 40000

Last Reported Employment: Engineer, Highway Planning

Public Record Information

Lien Filed 03/93; Fulton CTY; Case or Other ID Number-32114; Amount-$26667; Class-State; Released 07/93; Verified 07/93

Bankruptcy Filed 12/92; Northern District Ct; Case or Other ID Number-673HC12; Liabilities-$15787; Personal; Individual; Discharged; Assets-$780

Satisfied Judgment Filed 07/94; Fulton CTY; Case or Other ID Number-898872; Defendant-Consumer; Amount-$8984; Plaintiff-ABC Real Estate; Satisfied 03/95; Verified 05/95

Collection Agency Account Information

Pro Coll (800) xxx-xxxx

Collection Reported 05/96; Assigned 09/93 to Pro Coll (800) XXX-XXXX Client - ABC Hospital; Amount-$978; Unpaid; Balance $978; Date of Last Activity 09/93; Individual Account; Account Number 787652JC

Credit Account Information

Company Name	Account Number	Whose Acct	Date Opened	Months Reviewed	Date of Last Activity	High Credit	Terms	Items as of Date Reported			Date Reported
								Balance	Past Due	Status	
[1]	[2]	[3]	[4]	[5]	[6]	[7]	[8]	[9]	[10]	[11]	[12]
Department St.	32514	J	10/86	36	9/97	$950		$0		R1	10/97
Bank	1004735	A	11/86	24	5/97	$750		$0		I1	4/97
Oil Company	541125	A	6/86	12	3/97	$500		$0		O1	4/97
Auto Finance	529778	I	5/85	48	12/96	$1100	$50	$300	$200	I5	4/97

Previous Payment History: 3 Times 30 days late; 4 Times 60 days late; 2 Times 90+ days late
Previous Status: 01/97 - I2; 02/97 - I3; 03/97 - I4

Companies that Requested your Credit File

09/06/97	Equifax - Disclosure	08/27/97	Department Store
07/29/97	PRM Bankcard	07/03/97	AM Bankcard
04/10/97	AR Department Store	12/31/96	Equifax - Disclosure ACIS 123456789

How to Read Your Credit File

This section includes your name, current and previous addresses and other identifying information reported by creditors.

This section includes public record items obtained from local, state and federal courts.

This section includes accounts that creditors have turned over to a collection agency.

This section contains both open and closed accounts.

- 1 The credit grantor reporting the information.
- 2 The account number reported by the credit grantor.
- 3 See explanation below.
- 4 The month and year the credit grantor opened the account.
- 5 Number of months account payment history has been reported.
- 6 The date of last payment, change or occurrence.
- 7 Highest amount charged or the credit limit.
- 8 Number of installments or monthly payment.
- 9 The amount owed as of the date reported.
- 10 The amount past due as of the date reported.
- 11 See explanation below.
- 12 Date of last account update.

This section includes a list of businesses that have received your credit file in the last 24 months.

Whose Account	Status Type of Account
Indicates who is responsible for the account and the type of participation you have with the account. J = Joint I = Individual U = Undesignated A = Authorized User T = Terminated M = Maker C = Co-Maker/Co-Signer B = On behalf of another person S = Shared	O = Open (entire balance due each month) R = Revolving (payment amount variable) I = Installment (fixed number of payments) **Timeliness of Payment** 0 = Approved not used; too new to rate 1 = Paid as agreed 2 = 30+ days past due 3 = 60+ days past due 4 = 90+ days past due 5 = Pays or paid 120+ days past the due date; or collection account 7 = Making regular payments under wage earner plan or similar arrangement 8 = Repossession 9 = Charged off to bad debt

Form 102631–8-98 USA

The following inquiries are NOT reported to businesses:

PRM - This type of inquiry means that only your name and address were given to a credit grantor so they could offer you an application for credit. (PRM inquiries remain on file for 12 months.)

AM or AR - These inquiries indicate a periodic review of your credit history by one of your creditors. (AM and AR inquiries remain on file for 12 months.)

EQUIFAX, ACIS or UPDATE - These inquiries indicate Equifax's activity in response to your request for either a copy of your credit file or a request for research.

PRM, AM, AR, Equifax, ACIS, Update and INQ - These inquiries do not appear on credit files businesses receive, only on copies provided to you.

Personal Identification Information:

Check every item for accuracy from your name and address to every digit in your social security number. Are all previous addresses listed, or is there a gap? This is important, if you have not listed an address and it shows up on the file an employer or creditor could consider that a red flag. Twenty years ago having several addresses may have been suspect, but today with people moving constantly because of employment transfers it is not unusual to have lived in two or three cities in five or seven years. It is also not unreasonable to have lived in more than one residence in one city. If prospective creditors are using the number of residencies you report as a measure of stability it could hurt your chances. Date of birth is also listed and this can be a point of discrimination for older creditors and those seeking employment. Any date of birth on the credit report is an open invitation to identity fraud.

Our Social Security number is so important to who we are. When I got my first card in the late fifties, it was printed on the card. This card is not to be used for identification purposes. Now everything we do is tracked by our Social Security Number. The credit report includes your name, current address, social security number, date of birth and previous addresses. Check this carefully because misinformation in this section could cause you serious problems. If you list different addresses than shown on the record for previous addresses it may be determined you are withholding information. For instance if you rented an apartment while attending school, but never applied for credit or even sent payments from that address you may not have listed that address. Your car payments may have been mailed from that address or you bought tires or had an automotive repair. Even though your parents paid the bill, or you paid the bill from a check with your school address on it, that address may appear on the billing information of the company you dealt with. If you made payments (even 90 days) you will show up with an account with history.

Many applications ask for previous addresses, if they don't mesh, this information can go against you.

Verify the last reported employment. They ask for your last reported employment, and it is very important that this is correct. Incorrect information can be of a disservice to you for employment application purposes and credit granting.

Request for verification and update:

The notice must include the name, address, and phone number of the information source. (You can dispute the inaccurate items with the source of the information.) If you tell anyone such as a creditor who reports to a CRA that you dispute an item, they may not report the information to a CRA without including a notice of your dispute. We don't search out things that will help us, let alone read the small print. We need to notify the source of the error in writing if it continues to report the information. To do so is a violation of the FCRA.

Common misinformation about your credit report, and the files in the report can lead to a very low score and risk. Credit reporting agencies do not recommend a credit application be accepted or rejected. Credit grantors make that decision based on your payment record and their own criteria. Their criteria often have built in mechanisms looking for only the highest incomes and they develop a ratio system based on many things. Some on the length of time you are employed at one place, how long you have lived at a residence and how often you have moved. They evaluate different criteria differently at each company and some have a very high point value placed on six or seven criteria. CRA's do not rate accounts; they only maintain records and provide the information on each new inquiry directly from the data base.

It is important for you to check your credit report, at least once a year. You don't want to be blindsided when you do apply for a mortgage or car loan by information that is incorrect. The CRA usually can fix mistakes in 30 days through investigation but it could take longer and it could prevent you from closing a deal or getting a good loan for that vehicle.

Many card companies would like you to believe that they are the only ones you can deal with, but that is not so. Don't be intimidated. Let them know you know your rights, and make it clear you will file a research request form or a complaint with the FTC or state attorney general.

The Research Request form allows you to give details of the information you believe is incorrect. The CRA will then check with the credit grantor, collection agency or public record source to see if any error has been reported. Information that cannot be verified will be removed from your file. If you and a credit grantor disagree on any information, you will need to resolve the dispute directly with the credit grantor who is the source of the information.

Because each credit grantor has established criteria for making credit decisions it is hard to know why they do not grant credit. Your credit report will answer many of the questions like why you were turned down for credit only if you have some understanding of the information on the report. The vocabulary of credit terms in the glossary will help you determine some of the methods and give you an understanding of the terms and how they may apply to you.

This goes to the heart of things, and really is an unfair situation. Your credit may appear to be perfect, but having too much credit or too many outstanding balances are examples of why your request for credit might be declined. Also the number of applications on your account in a 90 day period affect credit decisions.

Sometimes the decision is not even based directly on the credit file; for instance, you may not have been at your current residence or in your present job long enough. And with many of the applications offering 60 second processing it is cold data they are looking at when making decisions. If you have any questions about why you were not approved for credit, contact the credit grantor who turned you down for credit for an explanation.

What is listed as your last reported employment is actually the last employment reported by credit grantors. Employment information is typically reported from applications for credit and therefore is not regularly updated.

How the credit review works:

Upon the receipt of the dispute, the relevant information provided by you is considered and reviewed regarding the nature of your dispute. If that review does not resolve your dispute and further investigation is required, the CRA provides notification of your dispute, including the relevant information submitted, to the source that furnished the dispute information. The source reviews the information provided, conducts an investigation with respect to the disputed information, and reports the results you. Then a deletion or change is made to the credit file as appropriate based on the results of the investigation. The name, address, and the phone number of the furnisher of information contacted while processing our disputes is shown under the results of the investigation section on the cover letter that accompanies the copy of your revised credit file. (Your I.Q. has nothing to do with not understanding the credit maze.)

If you still disagree with an item after it has been verified, you may send a brief statement to the CRA not to exceed 100 words. Your statement will become part of your credit file and will be disclosed each time your credit file is accessed.

If the reinvestigation results in a change to or deletion of the information you are concerned about, or you submit a statement in accordance with the preceding paragraph, you have the right to request the CRA send your revised credit file to any company that received your credit file in the past six months for any purpose or the past two years for employment purposes.

Keeping good records is crucial when you have serious problems with your credit. It is important to keep track of your credit history. It will take seven years for a delinquent account to be removed from your credit history. However the process does not begin the first day the account is over due. For instance, if you miss a payment on January 5th, a 180 day period of delinquency starts. Whether your account is turned over to a collection agency or taken as a loss by your creditor it will take six months until July 5th before the seven year period begins. Late fees and over the limit fees will continue to mount, changing the amount you owe. It pays to stay on top of any issue that affects your money.

Points to Ponder

Avoid walk-in offers at the local mall for credit and a gift for applying.

Companies are selling credit as well as merchandise. They want to pull customers in. Offering a special discount on slow days is part of their plan. The cubic zirconia earrings offered by a jewelry store, or the duffel bag for signing up for a major automobile credit card are very inexpensive gimmicks the companies can afford.

When you are purchasing big ticket items, like appliances, cars, diamonds, and gold watches, the sales are made on commission. The sales clerks not only compete with each other for your purchase, they compete for your credit. Most stores that have in house credit will offer you a special deal, like an additional discount, or another item, just to get you to open an account. The bottom line is the rejections cost a pair of phony earrings. The approvals earn a new customer with an instant sale. As a bonus, the company now has a new customer with a $1,000 or more credit line.

One national jewelry store has a nationwide contest for new credit applications every month between the stores. The sales clerks kept track of every credit application. This company had a little program called Diamond Dollars. Each associate would pull out the number of cards she was entitled to out of a jewelry bag. The scratch offs had values from one to fifty dollars with most being in the five and ten range. Sales Associates often earned three hundred dollars or more towards the purchase of anything in the store. This plus a 40% discount allows the associate to purchase items for much lower than the sale price.

Every time you apply for credit a notation is made in your history. Rejections are not good for your credit potential. Sales people will keep offering discounts until they make the sale, but its set up that way, it is the credit as much as the item. Cash sales are not as well accepted as credit sales for big items because the items

***This application needs a magnifying glass to read –
this is really small print!***

sell at the face value. The 20 dollars out of every 100 that you pay in cash robs the company of interest. Credit over cash is big business.

Congratulations - You are Pre-approved - Just send us your money.

Read the terms-especially for the type of card offered: Signing your name to an agreement before you read the small print can tie you into very high fees in addition to the high interest. *You may earn, you could be eligible*, is language designed (double talk) to confuse you.

What is the offer?

What is the annual percentage rate?

What is the membership fee?

What do they charge you up front to obtain the card?

When you get this far, you know that the offer is of no interest to you. Read the small print regarding extra fees: Don't put your self in a box by accepting small limit credit cards. It doesn't make sense to carry around a dozen low limit cards.

Buyer Beware - Make sure you understand the full cost.

The following are examples of some of the many credit card proposals:

- *Maximum credit limit up to $1,500.00*
- *Respond by July 5, 2002.*
- *Your good standing allows us to offer you a new credit card account.*
- *No security deposit*
- *No savings account*
- *(See insert for details)*
- *You will enjoy a credit limit from $250 up to $1,500.*
- *Although it is typical for applicants to receive a $250 credit line, your credit status can give you up to a maximum of $1,500. Your initial credit limit will be reduced by $175.00 due to one time new account fees. Remember, at Our Credit Card Company a good credit performance deserves to be rewarded. As you maintain your account you can earn automatic credit limit increase reviews.*
- *Your personal credit card in the name of Jane Doe will be processed immediately upon receipt of the attached acceptance form. Complete the information requested below and return it*

with your $29.00 processing fee. (Add six dollars for Express Processing made payable to Our Credit Card Company). A postage paid envelope is provided for your convenience. Your completed acceptance form and Processing Fee must be received by July 5, 2002 in order for us to issue your cards. (Trust me the offers will keep coming)

• I thank you, We look forward to welcoming you as a new Our Credit Card Company Cardholder.

• P.S. Would you like to save money while traveling and receive discounts at national retailers? Join the optional PREMIUM Club today by initialing the box below. (See reverse side for additional information.)

• The pre-approved status of this offer is conditioned on your response to this offer on or before the reply date (better offers to come if you don't reply) . Satisfying the credit-worthiness criteria used to select you for this offer, bearing on your creditworthiness including income, employment and any other information provided on your acceptance certificate will entitle you to a credit limit up to $1,500 or at least two hundred dollars.

• Even if you do not qualify for our unsecured credit card we may offer you a secured card to meet your credit needs.

Often the pre-approved amount is in red ink, is this a Freudian slip? The above offers were made on the basis of a PRM inquiry, which means a Credit reporting agency gave the company a potential creditor's name and address. (These inquires are not reported to businesses and are only seen on your record by you for 12 months).

Using credit wisely

Shop for the best interest, the lowest fees: The invitation to apply offers are often mass mailings casting the net for new customers. They want your money (credit) as much as any other business. By promising very low or no interest, and a low balance transfer option they hope you will accept their invitation.

* Using credit wisely begins with choosing credit wisely. Don't limit yourself to one card but don't go overboard either. Credit lines or limits are not what is expensive, it is the debt you pay interest on not the potential. Having credit to fall back on when the need arises is much better than trying on the spur of the moment to get credit increases.

ANNUAL PERCENTAGE RATE FOR PURCHASES	9.9%
OTHER ANNUAL PERCENTAGE RATES	APR for Cash Advances 23.9% and Penalty APR 23.9% for Purchases; see explanation below.[1]
FEES FOR ISSUANCE OR AVAILABILITY OF CREDIT	Program Fee: $95.00 (one-time fee), Account Set-Up Fee: $29.00 (one-time fee), Annual Fee: $48.00, Participation Fee: $72.00 Annually[2], Additional Card Fee: $20.00 Annually (if applicable)
GRACE PERIOD FOR REPAYMENT OF BALANCES FOR PURCHASES	If you pay your previous balance in full on or before the due date shown on your previous statement you will have a grace period on purchases of 25 days (from the statement closing date to the payment due date), and can avoid finance charges on current purchases by paying the statement in full on or before the due date.

METHOD OF COMPUTING BALANCE FOR PURCHASES	Average Daily Balance (Including new purchases)
MINIMUM FINANCE CHARGE	$0.50
TRANSACTION FEE FOR CASH ADVANCES	Greater of $5.00 or 3% of the amount of the cash advance
FEES FOR PAYING LATE OR EXCEEDING THE CREDIT LIMIT	Late Payment Fee: $25 each time the payment is late. Over Limit Fee: $25 each month the balance exceeds the credit limit.

[2]The Participation Fee of $72.00 will be billed at $6.00 per month.

Other Fees: Return Item Charge: $25.00, Auto Draft Charge: $5.00/$3.00* per draft, Express Delivery Fee: $25.00 for card(s) sent Express Mail, Copying Fee $3.00 per item, Credit Limit Increase Fee: $25.00 the first time we approve an increase.

[1]**Penalty Pricing Information:** If your Account goes past the due date two times in any six month period or goes past the due date for two consecutive billings cycles, the APR will increase to 23.9%. The APR will be reduced back to 9.9% if the Account is kept current for 3 consecutive months or is paid in full.

Account Terms: This credit card Account ("Account") is offered and credit cards are issued by ███████ Bank ███████. When your account is approved, the complete terms applicable to the Account will be furnished to you with the card. In the following disclosures, "Bank", "we", "our" and "us" each refer to ███████ Bank, and "you" and "your" each refer to the person applying to us for an Account.

Fair Credit Reporting Act Notice: Information contained in a credit bureau report received from a credit reporting agency was used by us in connection with this offer of credit. You received this offer because that report indicated that you satisfied certain criteria for credit worthiness used to select consumers for this offer. The credit may not be extended or you may be offered an alternative credit product if, after you respond to this offer, we determine, that the credit bureau was incorrect; that you no longer meet the criteria used to select you for this offer; or that, based upon information provided in your request for credit, you do not meet other criteria bearing on credit worthiness we have established for this offer. You have the right to prohibit the use of information contained in your credit file with any credit reporting agency for all future credit transactions that are not initiated by you. You may exercise this right by calling ███████ or by writing these agencies.

Available Credit: The Program Fee of $95.00, the Annual Fee of $48.00, Account Set-up Fee of $29.00, Additional Card Fee of $20.00 (if applicable) and monthly Participation Fee of $6.00 will appear on your first billing statement. These fees will reduce your available credit until they are paid.

FINANCE CHARGES: Your Account will also be subject to the following FINANCE CHARGES, each of which will be billed to your Account as a purchase:

Periodic FINANCE CHARGES: FINANCE CHARGES are imposed when you obtain a cash advance and when a purchase is posted to your Account. FINANCE CHARGES are imposed from the time a purchase is posted until it is paid in full. However, if you pay your previous balance in full on or before the payment due date shown on your previous statement, you will have a grace period on purchases of twenty-five (25) days (from the statement closing date to the payment due date) and can avoid FINANCE CHARGES on current purchases by paying the current statement in full on or before that payment due date. FINANCE CHARGES are imposed on cash advances from the date the advance is made until it is paid in full and there is no grace period in which you may repay a cash advance to avoid FINANCE CHARGES.

Computing Periodic FINANCE CHARGES: The FINANCE CHARGE is determined by multiplying the "Average Daily Balance" for purchases and for cash advances outstanding during the monthly billing cycle by the monthly "Periodic Rate." The monthly "Periodic Rate" for purchases is .825%, which is equivalent to an ANNUAL PERCENTAGE RATE of 9.9%. The monthly "Periodic Rate" for penalty pricing for purchases is 1.991%, which is equivalent to an ANNUAL PERCENTAGE RATE of 23.9%. The monthly "Periodic Rate" for cash advances is 1.991%, which is equivalent to an ANNUAL PERCENTAGE RATE of 23.9%. The "Average Daily Balance" is computed by taking the beginning balance of your Account on each day, calculated separately for purchases

and cash advances, adding new purchases and/or cash advances and subtracting any payments or credits to get each day's daily balance. The daily balances are then added together and divided by the number of days in the billing cycle to get the "Average Daily Balance." The minimum FINANCE CHARGE is $.50 for each billing cycle during which a FINANCE CHARGE based upon a periodic rate is imposed.

Cash Advance Fee: In addition to the monthly calculation of the cash advance FINANCE CHARGE, there is an additional FINANCE CHARGE of the greater of $5.00 or 3% of the amount of cash advance for each cash advance obtained that month.

Program Fee: We impose a one-time Program Fee of $95.00 to your Account as a condition of extending credit to you. The Program Fee is a FINANCE CHARGE.

Account Set-up Fee: We impose a one time Account Set-up Fee of $29.00 as a condition of extending credit to you. This fee is a FINANCE CHARGE.

Credit Limit Increase Fee: When we approve your Account for an unsecured credit limit increase, a Credit Limit Increase Fee of $25.00 is imposed. This is a one-time fee, which is assessed only with the first approval of your credit limit increase. This is a FINANCE CHARGE.

Express Delivery Fee: We impose a $25.00 fee for the express delivery of your Card sent priority 2-day airmail. This fee is a FINANCE CHARGE.

Auto Draft Charge: We impose a $9.00 charge for each payment you request be made through an auto draft service we provide. Auto draft payments requested through our automated systems (i.e. Voice Response or Internet) are assessed $5.00 per transaction. This fee is a FINANCE CHARGE.

Authorization: You certify that all information given in this form is true and correct and you are giving this information in order to obtain credit and authorize the Bank to obtain information concerning any statements herein. You agree to furnish the Bank with all requested information. You authorize the Bank to charge the Annual Fee, Program Fee, Account Set-Up Fee, the Additional Card Fee (if applicable) and the monthly Participation Fees to your Account.

Qualify For Future Credit Limit Increases: You will be eligible for consideration for a credit limit increase after 6 months. Initially, you will be issued a ███████ with at least a $250.00 credit limit up to a maximum of $1,000.00. This program is designed to allow individuals to increase their credit limit by establishing creditworthiness with ███████ Bank.

Refund Disclosure: When your Account is approved, you will be sent a cardholder contract containing all of the terms applicable to your Account. If you elect to close your Account(s) within 30 days of receiving your cardholder contract and before you make any additional charges to the card the Annual Fee, Account Set Up Fee, Program Fee, monthly Participation Fee and Additional Card Fee (if applicable) will be refunded to you. After this 30 day period these fees are no longer refundable and you are responsible for the account.

ARBITRATION: If you are issued a credit card, your cardholder contract will contain a binding arbitration provision. In the event of any dispute relating to your credit card or cardholder contract, the dispute will be resolved by binding arbitration pursuant to the rules of the National Arbitration Association and both you and we agree to waive the right to go to court or to have the dispute heard by a jury (except in regard to any collection activities on your account). You and we will be waiving any right to a jury trial and you also would not have the right to participate as part of a class of claimants relating to any dispute with us. Other rights available to you in court may also be unavailable in arbitration. When you receive your cardholder contract you should read the arbitration provision in your contract carefully and not accept or use the card unless you agree to be bound by the arbitration provision.

If you have questions regarding this application, please write us at ███████ Bank, ███████. Member FDIC.

For Additional Disclosures please refer to the enclosed insert.

When you receive a credit card offer you are interested in, instead of mailing your credit application, apply over the phone. If you apply by phone you can get a lot more information about the terms of the card. Also usually you will get an answer right away. It is too risky to mail information in response to an invitation to apply. Even if the company is one you know and trust, it is better to make the connection with the company by phone. Don't apply on line through an advertisement on the internet. The company you think you are applying to may have one little letter different in the name and be a totally different company. Do as much as you can on line, but only after you establish a relationship with the bank or merchant. If you want to take advantage of balance transfer offers with very low interest don't send information through the mail. These companies are waiting for your call. When you are approved they will do everything they can to allow you to take full advantage of the offer. Because down the road your potential for credit with them is a sure thing.

A MasterCard or VISA, American Express (30 day balance card) Discover, (cash back card) gasoline card, and one or two department store cards will give you flexible spending options that will help you have the cash flow for living expenditures. Notice I said living expenses not all the pie in the sky stuff you want. It is really important to put a harness on your wants. If you can only buy them on credit, then you can't afford them. Designate the use of the cards for certain areas of expenditures. It is wise to have a card at one of the big nationwide department stores (Sears or J.C. Penny) that offer an automotive center, home decorating, large appliances, and clothing. K-Mart and Wal-Mart are also to be considered because of the services they offer besides the merchandise. You should build your good credit history by planning the use of credit as you meet your living expenses and develop your savings. Establish a credit ceiling and create a plan for lowering your debt instead of recycling your debt. **Never buy groceries on credit.** Use your debit card or cash at restaurants. If you do use a credit card, don't add the tip to the card. Do everything you can to cut down fees and interest. Buying food on credit, unless you are expensing for business is a poor choice.

Use your gasoline card for gas, and other things for the car. Many cards have bonus programs. If you buy so many gallons a month, they offer a coupon for free gas. Keep track of your expenditures. When you stop at the gas station to fill up, and buy snacks and drinks for yourself and your family, don't put it on the card. Think about it; that extra ten dollars a couple of times a month on your credit card, is raising the interest.

Don't use convenience checks.

When you get those little convenience checks with your statement, again don't treat it like money found. It is credit, a cash advance. The credit card company wants you to think this is extra cash to pay bills when you are tight. Sounds like a good idea, but it is not. At Christmas time it would be a lot smarter to use your card for purchases and forget the checks. Don't use the checks to pay other bills, all you are doing is increasing your debt, and your interest. This is the best scheme I ever heard of "To rob Peter to pay Paul", and it will catch up with you.

Avoid cash advances on credit cards.

This is another option that seems like a good idea at the time. Being able to get cash whenever you need it, regardless of how much interest you pay back is a false sense of security. Besides paying a service fee to your creditor, you also pay a service charge to the bank from which you make the ATM withdrawal. It seems a little weird to me that they keep offering us all this money. We pay them back at a high interest rate, and they still charge us service fees. Also you will notice on your account statement, cash withdrawals are listed as a separate item. Often the amount towards the cash advance is very low, drags out over many months, and the interest ends up being much higher.

• Use your credit card to make large routine payments like insurance for the car or renter's insurance. Insurance payments usually put a big dent on every budget. If one thing happens to cause an immediate financial need, the payment is short. This is why you should keep your credit potential high and use it for big payments. If you set up a schedule where you pay your automobile insurance by credit card, and pay that off in 90 days, it will be much easier. The thing that often happens is people make that big payment, then live off their credit cards until the next payday. When you are broke you are vulnerable. One payment instead of many, while trying to meet several needs will ease that vulnerability.

• Carefully track your payments and interest charges: If you pay only the minimum payment every month, you are increasing the debt each month. Keep your credit expenditures under one third of your income, and with an open balance of at least one half of your credit line. Watch those interest payments. On a balance of a thousand dollars, the interest will be higher than the payment. The creditor isn't thinking of your well being when he sets a payment low. He wants you to feel secure and at ease in meeting the payment, and hoping you won't notice that your interest is increased, sometimes double your monthly payment. Set up a payment schedule to show the balance diminishing. If your payment is low, $15 or $20, make a double payment plus the interest.

• If there are times when you can't do this, pay the interest accrued for that month instead of the monthly payment. If you pay the interest each month as your payment you will make more headway than paying the bare minimum.

• Carefully study any offers for insurance coverage and credit card protection against theft of your cards. This is usually a telemarketing scheme. This is where reading the small print is very important. Insurance sounds good and they make you feel like you are very responsible when you accept this. The chance of you ever collecting coverage is very low. A death benefit that will goes directly to the company to pay off your account is often the main benefit. Also you are foolish to buy protection for all your credit cards with every company you deal with.

• Pick and choose carefully. They all want your money. It is up to you to decide if they are worthy of your credit, instead of the other way around.

• A credit line is not found money. Learn to manage not max out!

How many books, CD's and videos are sitting in the corner unopened?

Many people don't consider book clubs a form of credit, but it is. It is also an avenue to give away your name and address for a few dollars in savings to every catalog and membership vendor.

Read the small print. You are obligated for so many books over a period of time. What they don't tell you is they may send about three notices a month, often with short turn around. If you don't pay attention to anything else I say listen to this. When you have a dispute (with book company or bank) you need to enter that dispute immediately.

When you send in a notice, either accepting or rejecting an offer, mark it on your calendar. Open the items when they arrive. The CD or video you are waiting for as a gift, may not be the one that you receive. If you wait until you need the gift, the surprise will be on you. Make sure the correct item is in the package when you receive your order. Many book and CD companies do not have customer service numbers. You may not be able to get a replacement order in time to give the gift when dealing with snail mail.

When you receive packages from a club check the calendar, if you are not waiting for anything, return it. If you open the package and you don't want it, you will have to pay the return postage.

Sometimes it can take months to get your account straight. Resign yourself to giving in to the hassle, if you don't, you will end up paying for a lot of product you don't want.

What you don't need now, lay-away:

Lay-away is the best tool you have to keep those credit card balances low. It is a tremendous antidote to binge buying and mismanaging debt. When you run into the discount store to buy a last minute gift for a child's party, and you see a sale on TVs, put the TV on layaway not a credit card.

Payday Loans

Payday loans were highly criticized during the last presidential election by the consumer advocate candidate because of the high interest rates charged for a short term loan. If you strictly base the cost of the loan on the fee and determine the fee as APR, the rate will look much higher than it actually is because you are paying for a loan each time you receive new money and not carrying the loan. Loan rates and fees vary with each state and you need to read the agreement before you sign it.

People's Choice a check cashing and payday outlet in Kansas offers loans up to $200.00 (the pay back is $219.00) for a two week period on the presentation of a personal check covering the loan and the fee. The personal check is the collateral and if it bounces you will pay overdraft fees to your bank. The lender's overdraft fees will be much higher than the loan fee.

When the debt comes due, the borrower has the option to buy back the check or run it through their account. Once the borrower gives the money to cover the $219 loan, he can get a new loan in the same amount and the same conditions.

This fee is much higher than the service charge at an ATM for a cash advance on your credit or debit card. It is much lower than overdraft charges you will pay if you can't cover a check for unexpected expenses. Giving yourself two weeks to clear the check is a lot smarter than trying to beat your next deposit.

If you roll over a $200 loan twenty six times a year, the up front cost is $494.00 for a total cash advance of $5,200.00. If you take cash advances from your credit card in the same amount every two weeks, making a payment just to cover the advance so you can do it again, you are paying service fees and compound interest.

Use this option with restraint, don't use payday loans for entertainment or things you know you can't afford.

Watch those fees

Don't risk late payments or overdraft charges. Make sure you don't mail payments early. A simple mistake in your checking account can be very costly. Many years ago I wrote out my checks to mail out the following Saturday after I deposited my pay check. I had three utility bills, water, electric and phone, and one department store bill. A couple of days later when I went to add another bill to the collection I discovered the envelopes were gone. My daughter gleefully announced to me that she mailed my letters for me. The next morning I each called each place of business and explained the situation. Even the department store was very understanding, the checks were held, and not deposited. With today's payment centers from utility companies to credit card companies, we can't count on getting through. Even if we did, the chances are we would not be able to stall a deposit. Big business is too big today to cover a small mistake.

Several years later I went through a similar situation. On the way home from work I made a deposit (my income tax refund) at the drive in window. I had the deposit slip documentation showing the transaction. It wasn't until seven days later, when I started getting NSF notices, that I discovered the deposit was not credited to my account. I called the bank immediately and after they argued with me for five minutes about it not being possible that they made that mistake, they told me I had to contact IRS. A habit developed several years earlier of writing down the number of my allotment check had been carried through on all government and pay checks. It paid off because by the end of the day IRS verified to the bank the check had been cashed. The bank made good on each overdraft charge and paid all the checks. It actually took only three weeks and letters from the bank to clear the account.

Identity Theft

Nothing can happen to you financially that can cause more personal destruction and long term damage to your lifestyle and your credit history than identity theft. Identity theft has the push and power of a tornado or hurricane, and there are very few resources to deal with it. Once you discover unauthorized purchases and transactions on various accounts are happening it could be way beyond the reconcilable period.

Identity theft can happen to you and it is not as difficult as you think. Your financial information can be illegally obtained by both friends and foe, and even relatives that have access to your personal information.

Years ago I had my social security number on my checks. A friend of mine who also worked at my bank told me never to order things by catalog or from TV ads with a personal check. After thinking about her warning, I realized not only do you give up your account number and routing information, but also your address, phone number and social security number.

The rich have the resources to cover the expense of identity fraud and can bring the matter to close much quicker than the average consumer. Identity fraud can leave your finances and your life in shambles for years to come causing severe losses that will take you years to recover.

As soon as you have any indication or evidence that some one is using your checking account or credit card accounts put a security alert on your credit report with all three CRAs. This alert will stay on your report 60 days and it should stay on much longer than that, because it is impossible to know all the ramifications during a 60 day period. Also we should not have to pay for a service from the CRAs to help us prevent identity fraud. As long as CRAs have full control over our records by selling information for unsolicited credit we are at risk of identity fraud.

Identity thieves are brutal and very clever. They can put in a change of address with the post office for your personal mail for a short period of time, to gain access to all your account numbers and financial statements. This enables them to open new accounts in your name and withdraw funds from money market accounts and other savings accounts.

Fixing the problems that result from identity fraud will take more than a phone call or two. It could take months, even years and tons of documentation to clear your name and credit history of bad debt notations. It won't be an easy task and you will feel violated, embarrassed and angry a hundred times over. You will have to present a mountain of paper work to each and every credit card company, lender and financial institution where your accounts were invaded.

Resolve in your own mind that you will do everything to regain your credibility and discharge debts you did not incur. Besides the security alert place a statement in your credit file regarding the identity theft activity. Contact your creditors and banks immediately to inform them of this activity. Call then back up the call with written notice.

Contact the Federal Trade Commission for guidelines on how to begin dealing with Identity Fraud. Contact your state attorney general and hire a lawyer and even an accountant. Trying to file all the paper work and pull together all the records for necessary is not wise. Your creditors will pay more attention to your claims when they know you are pursuing this through channels.

Be prepared to press charges against the individuals that ruined your credit, and caused serious damage as well as heavy financial loss. Even if you learn the thief is not a stranger but some one you know or are related to you must press charges. If you don't press charges it may be very difficult to pursue the necessary relief through the courts that will recover good credit history and discharge the bad debt you are not responsible for.

Check the billing dates and the date your check cleared.

Call the creditor as soon as you receive your statement (this is why it is important to open the statement when it comes). It may be necessary to speak with a supervisor at the onset because the operator may try and convince you the mistake is yours. If you have been charged a late fee or any other fees it is up to you to present documentation that your payment beat the closing date.

Even if the mistake had been yours, the customer is supposed to be right. Most of us just don't want to spend time fighting with people about mistakes we didn't make. When it is a small dollar amount sometimes we think it's not worth it just not to get involved. It is always worth the time, so take it.

Opting Out

Most states have passed laws to protect us from the intrusion of telemarketing. The problem is the process takes so long to take effect it sometimes seems like its almost as much of an annoyance as receiving the calls. It begins with signing (or submitting your request through an 800 number provided by the state attorney general) an opt out form similar to form from the CRAs to get your name off the solicitation list. It is just one more thing that we have to attend to in order to protect our privacy. Signing the form does not make it a done deal, companies will still call. It is just one of those nagging little things that you will have to carry through on, even if it means filing a formal complaint against the company. Any calls with solicitations on your answering machine, whether it's a charity request or an offer for a free dream vacation should be reported to the attorney. This takes time. The telemarketing companies are betting we won't take the time. Many of the telemarketing calls we have received are just recorded messages.

This also goes to the issue of the people you do business with that sell your name, address and phone number to other business-es. Don't you just love the special offers you get that come addressed to the resident or current resident. When you change residences or if you are having problems with a lot of telemarketing and junk mail solicitations, call your local phone company and request your personal information not be sold on lists to any vendors.

In many states there is an option to sign on the first phone bill for new service to keep your name off of lists. Most of the time you won't be able to prove your name was sold by an entity unless you have the bizarre experience I had with the book club that messed my name up completely. Even though I straightened it out with the book club, I received several direct offers for credit cards with the phony name. It takes too much time to deal with this and get your name off lists, and there is no guarantee that your name will stay off lists if you move out of your current residence area to another state.

Once companies have a phone number they could care less who actually owns that number. For the past three years I have received calls for a family that has not had this number for five years. When you tell the caller that Mrs. So and So does not live here, they just go right on with their spiel asking if you are the lady of the house or the homeowner. During the day when I am working

I screen the calls through the answering machine. The long message while sometimes annoying to my friends, stating who doesn't live here is still not a deterrent for the recorded messages. Getting rid of the telemarketing calls and snail mail offers is just one more responsibility put on us that we could be using the time for more useful purposes. However, unless you put forth the effort, regardless of the time involvement you can say good by to any peace of mind at the dinner table or otherwise.

> ### *"In late December of 2002 the Federal Trade Commission announced a no call national registry plan."*

Privacy Peril

Unsolicited credit card offers are a nuisance. Consumers have the right under the law to opt out of unsolicited offers by calling an 800 number. If you request a form from the CRA you can have your name removed indefinitely. Does "indefinitely" mean seven years, or until you move from your current address?

The consumer would be afforded much better protection and service if they could opt in. That is give the CRA's the right to sell their name and address. As consumers we have no control over the selling of our information to creditors, but we should have the absolute right to have our name and address proffered out to the highest bidder.

Even though I have opted out by calling the 800 number, I have received a hundred twenty three unsolicited offers from one bank since October 15, 1999. The offers were mailed to two different addresses and under three different names.

Although I kept the same phone number and had signed not to have my name and address sold by the phone company, it was. Shortly after I moved into my new address I joined a book club. Again signing the option not to have my name sold.

About 75 percent of my mail comes addressed to the name on the cover of this book. That is exactly how my name appears on my checking account, debit card and several credit cards.

The name on my phone bill is simply first, middle initial and last name. But it is the third name that is very interesting. I am not sure whether the book club couldn't read my writing, (or printing) or the data entry person was talking on the phone with someone else when she entered my name and address. It took me ten months to get my name changed from Faan Heenan to Fran Hernan. In the meantime I received several (over 50) unsolicited offers from book clubs, mail order catalogs (many with pre-approved credit offers for up to $500). I was getting the offers under all three names from several credit cards, sometimes all in the same day.

Besides the inconvenience and annoyance, there is a real threat. The offers changed with lower interest rates each time they came, but the ironic thing is, the fictitious name is the one that consistently received the best offers.

Because I was gathering research for this book, I kept every offer I received. The normal thing to do is throw them away. If you don't cut them up in little pieces or shred each offer, you are putting your self at risk. It is ridiculous to think that our privacy has been invaded to the point that we have to take time to destroy credit offers we would never accept.

Another curious thing about these offers, something I can't prove, but am very suspicious about. Living at my daughters, with my own phone for two years I received one credit card offer. As soon as I moved I started receiving offers for secured accounts and non- secured accounts! Why? Is it possible when the companies buy information they have a way of targeting what they think is low income or an inner city area? I moved into an apartment complex six blocks from City Hall and the Federal Court House. It is very hard to explain, but this once little town has grown by leaps and bounds without creating the typical down town syndrome.

Choosing a Lender & the Loan you need

A friend of mine said recently, "a bank only wants to lend you money when you don't need it."

We know that spending beyond our limits is very dangerous, but many of us have never sat down and examined and evaluated our past expenses and carefully prepared a budget for day to day living. You have to know how much you have, how much you need and how much you spend.

Government figures show many households are spending more than they make. If you are making $50,000 a year, and spending $60,000 and don't have protection in terms of health insurance, renter's insurance and a minimum life insurance you are a candidate for financial disaster. You could be paying horrific interest rates for everything the rest of your life, or end up filing bankruptcy. If you don't wise up and get help. Learn to control spending and understand you have the ability to change your finances.

Once you have made the decision to seek a loan, get your mortgage papers along with insurance, tax and other documents together. Draw a line down the middle of a yellow legal pad. On the left side go through your mortgage papers and itemize the terms, monthly payment, points, length of loan, interest rate(APR). Identify the type of loan you have and the type of loan you want to apply for.

First you need to decide the type of loan you are going to apply for. Is it a first mortgage, second mortgage, refinancing for lower interest or loan to value of the property, (home equity loan), and what is the amount of the loan you need. Shop around to find the best deal. If you settled on a second mortgage or a loan to lower your interest, contact your current lender first. If there is something in your history that prevents you from getting the rate you want from your current lender, then start looking elsewhere. Interest rates, fees and points that go into making up the cost of the loan can vary quite a bit between full service banks, savings and loans, credit unions and mortgage companies.

Lower interest refinancing.

First of all you need to decide what you want. Do you want to simply refinance your home to take advantage of the lower interest rates? To do so could mean a savings of tens of thousands of dollars over the life of the mortgage. However, you would have to go through the same process you went through when you applied for your mortgage. This includes getting an appraisal, buying points, title search, property taxes and insurance. Every step you took with the first mortgage will be repeated including paying the closing costs.

If you decide you can afford the up front cost of refinancing by all means look into it. The first place to start is your bank or the lender that issued the first mortgage. Be prepared to go through a credit check. Your current credit history will determine your risk factor and your ability to pay back the new loan.

Refinancing strictly to lower your interest and payments may be the best option you have. But it does involve up front fees. Before you start thinking about what lender you will choose, determine what kind of loan you need. Separate the refinancing from the second mortgage and the Home Equity loan.

If you are going to embark on a big financial transaction that involves a savings of tens of thousands of dollars make sure in fact that it does. Hire a competent attorney. Whatever you spend in this manner will protect you from rushing in and not making the best deal. If you have a 15 year fixed rate loan, and have been paying back that loan for ten and a half years, refinancing may not make as much sense as it would if you the loan was six years old. In this case other needs could be the determining factor.

Things you need to know about the lender and the loan you are applying for:

Interest Rate: A word of caution about this, when you apply on line or by phone write down the exact interest percentage and compare it to the decimal point when you get the forms. If there is a change don't accept it. The lender is obligated to give you the interest they quoted. If the interest quoted was a mistake or the interest went up, you need to negotiate a percentage that is not way out of line with the initial rate. Don't let the lender talk you into accepting the higher rate by saying the difference is really very small and it is based on new rates. Over 30 years it can be considerable. Consider the value of face to face contact with a local lender.

Points: How many points do you have to pay? This is part of the Annual Percentage Rate (APR) but you need a break down of every charge,

Fees: What are fees attached to the loan? When are you responsible for the fees? If you finance the fees as part of the loan you pay additional interest for the life of the loan. When the lender offers a no closing cost option it usually means the closing costs are included in the loan. Points and fees added to the loan means you are paying more interest over the term of the loan. Before you consider adding these fees, do a little math. Is it much different paying off a credit card balance in the amount of $3,000 with the loan proceeds than adding $3,000 to your loan amount and paying interest at a lower rate? Don't fall victim to the double talk.

What is the term of the loan?

Watch this. Remember a longer term may mean lower payments each month, but you will pay more interest and take longer to reduce the loan. What are the monthly payments? Do the payments go for both interest and the principal of the loan? Don't sign up for an interest only loan unless you are certain you can make a balloon payment at the end of the loan for the full amount of the loan.

Shop around.

Before you put your biggest asset and most prized possession in the hands of strangers, explore your options.

Combined Loan to Value, is the relationship between the unpaid principal balances of all the mortgages on a property and the property's appraised value.

Home equity loans are costly cash that could destroy your financial well being. If you are having trouble paying bills and see no end in sight, why would you risk the thing that is most important to you? If your credit is in such bad shape that the obligations are affecting your lifestyle severely, why is getting deeper in debt even an option? Smaller payments will give you more monthly cash, but if it extends the loan or costs more in interest is it worth it? Be sure before you jump!

Home Improvement Loans.

On the other hand, home equity loans to improve or add on to your home may not be a bad idea, if the improvement adds to the appreciation of the property. Several years ago when I was looking for a house close to my work, a friend told me about a place within walking distance. A friend of his had built the house for his mother but she never moved in. At first the owner said he wasn't interested in renting it. He called back two weeks later and offered to rent the house.

The house was a very nice one story, three bedroom. Everything in it was beautiful. The custom kitchen was gorgeous. There were two big bathrooms, but both had showers and no tubs. There was only one door, no back door. (I worked in the building department of this little town, and even my boss couldn't explain how that got by the planners). We could have probably made adjustments, my boss even said he would put in a back door for me. So why didn't I jump at the house? The beautiful wall to wall plush carpet was fuchsia.

That house stayed vacant until they finally sold it, and I am told the carpet was replaced before they put it on the market. The point of this story is simple. When you spend several thousand dollars on improvements for your home be sure the improvements have a value for resale of the house.

Home equity generated line of credit.

The basic rules when applying for, or using any of the credit you already have should depend on needs. Before you sign, be very sure you aren't giving up much more than you are getting. If you need to consider an equity loan because of a life event that has thrown your finances and emotional domains into chaos, getting a high interest loan to pay off medical bills may be reasonable if you don't let your emotions run away with you.

NOTE: *A home equity loan is not a windfall, it is a passport to unforgivable debt. There is no better way to increase your financial vulnerability and create a high risk rating if you don't put the proceeds of your loan towards high interest debt, that will stay with you. A life event, like a sudden death in the* *family, a catastrophic illness or unemployment, life events and not just material things that we sometimes think impact the quality of our life much more than it does. 2001 saw record shattering mortgage refinancing (Peter Miller-Homeownership Alliance)*

Getting a line of credit on your equity is akin to playing Russian roulette where an unexpected life event could pull the trigger. If you can't meet payments and live within your means now what happens when your company folds? This economy is not painting a picture of full employment from one end of the country to the other.

Truth in lending.

The creditor must give you written notice of your right to cancel, and if you decide to cancel you must notify the creditor in writing within the three day period. The creditor must then return all fees paid and cancel the security interest in your home.

A contractor can't start working on your home or be paid by the lender until the three days are up. If you must have the cash immediately to meet a financial emergency, you may give up your right to cancel by providing a written explanation of the circumstances. Don't be pressured. There is no emergency that you can't forestall at least three days if you can promise cash payment.

The right to cancel (or right of rescission) is provided to protect you against hasty decisions made under pressure that might put your home at risk. If you give up your rights on Wednesday and lose your job on Thursday, you have no recourse.

The creditor is obligated to give you written notice of your right to cancel and if he doesn't offer it, be sure you remind him. When you decide to cancel, you must give the creditor a notice in writing within the three-day period. Either hand carry, fax or send it by registered mail special delivery to make certain the notice is delivered before midnight of the third day of the waiting period. The lender that comes to your door to have you sign for the loan cannot be expected to come to your home to pick up this notice. This right to cancel is provided to the consumer to protect you from hasty decisions and decisions made under pressure. Once the creditor receives this notice all fees paid must be returned and the creditor must cancel the security interest in your home within twenty days.

Before you go through with the loan you should have your attorney look at the loan papers.

The Right of Rescission does not apply to a first mortgage to finance the purchase of a home. You commit yourself as soon as you sign the mortgage contract.

Under the law you can waive your right to rescind if you have the need for funds immediately because of damage from a natural disaster. A statement (signed by you and anyone that shares interest in the property waiving your right) must be signed and dated and presented to the creditor.

Owning a home is the American dream, don't turn it into a nightmare that causes the loss of your home.

Never Sign Over Your Deed

It is absolutely amazing at the number of borrowers who are duped into this action. It is just one more piece of evidence towards the vulnerability people feel when they have made some bad choices as they try to get out of financial trouble. Don't trust strangers. It is like a shell game, you get behind on the loan, another company comes in, offers to help but needs your deed to secure the funds to pay off the other company. Now you are in their hands, and whether you make the payments or not, essentially what you are doing is renting your own home. The temporary measure to prevent foreclosure is a tool lenders use as a carrot, the carrot keeps moving until it is out of sight, the refinancing never comes through and what is yours is now his. He can borrow on it; he can sell it with the proceeds going to him, not you. Your mortgage payments become rent, and your mortgage payments include the insurance and taxes, so he has everything, and you are paying into building up the equity again for him, not you. If your rent is late you can lose your home. Be careful not to sign a document that gives him certain rights, like keeping some of your possessions in lieu of the late payments.

It is important to contact your attorney when considering such an important legal undertaking. Unfortunately, home owners may not understand this when they enter into the home equity loan process. If you think you can't afford an attorney to review the documents, it might be a sign you can't afford the high risk of the loan at this time.

Put Your Pride Aside

Go ahead, feel guilty, then rationalize, blame the mess on your spouse, or your mother in law. Get the kids in on the act too, but remember you are the one responsible for making choices when it goes to needs and wants. Don't start projecting about the future or how much your kids will hate you.

If this doesn't help go ahead have a pity party, feel as sorry for yourself as you can . . . OK, time is up.

On to recovery through responsibility, figuring out just where you are so you determine how to get on track emotionally and financially.

Don't throw the bills against the wall to see what lands on the top of the pile. It doesn't matter how you got here. You are here. No road map, no resources or at least that is the feeling. There has to be a way to get back on the road to life without debt overcoming you completely.

Before you decide on a plan that involves outside help you need to review your income and out go. To do this, much like in the first section you need to determine what you have. The parameters are a little different, tomorrow is the only future you can think about.

Cut up the credit cards, learn to regulate your spending. Pay attention to the little things that add up. Once you come to the conclusion that you can't continue like you have been, develop a strategy to get you back on track. Part of the strategy may be to think about today rather than tomorrow. Put savings on the back burner.

Consider this until you rein in the outrageous interest debt you have incurred. Do you have any savings at all? Do your children have several hundred dollars worth of savings bonds, or a passbook account? It isn't stealing and you will pay it back, with interest. Instead of letting the money sit, use it to get out of the bind you find yourself in. Every effort you make to get past the financial road blocks will ease the load.

I hate the words *giving up* and *sacrifice* but you may have to do a lot of that in the next six months. The first thing you have to give up, is the bad habit of spending automatically for things you don't need. But even more important you need to keep records of what you spend and what you have.

List all your fixed expenditures, beginning with rent, utilities, car payments, insurance, phone and cable. Subtract this from your spendable income.

Now to the next step of trying to figure out how you can increase your cash flow by taking steps to reduce your expenditures.

Examine your tax deductions.

Now is the time to look at your withholding. Take every deduction you are entitled to for at least the next six months. A hundred dollars a month now instead of a big return next year, might be the difference between having the phone turned off or keeping the service.

Even out your expenditures.

You know you have to pay utilities every month. Knowing exactly what you have to pay will give you the freedom to plan the expenditures and take away the fear of losing the utilities because you can't pay a large heating bill the month after Christmas. In the long run, low bills a couple of months in the summer will not give you any real financial freedom. Check out the budget or average pay plan offered by your local utility companies.

Evaluate all fixed expenses:

Any services you have on contract, like cell phones, could incur additional expenses if you try to give them up. Look for ways to cut back with out giving up completely.

Do you need caller ID, if you do keep it? Do you need call waiting or call notes? Determine exactly what services you need. Don't let the customer service representative talk you into keeping the services because you are getting such a good deal with the combination of services. If you save twenty five or thirty dollars a month on services you don't need, you can spend it on things you do need. $30.00 a month can put a dent in school supplies. Increasing your cash flow even by a few dollars a month can ease the tension of not being able to meet expenses.

Evaluate each incidental expense, internet service, switching from DSL to dial up could save thirty or forty dollars. If you have not watched a premium channel in several months, cut them. Don't interrupt the family channels or the Disney channel that the kids live for in their free time.

List your accounts as follows:
Lender and Card name:
Date opened (year is enough):
Balance:
Open Credit:
Due Date:
Payment amount:

Under payment amount list the payment status, any late fees or other charges for that account on the current statement.

Categorize each account to the best of your ability according to the statement information.

Current, 30 days past due 60 days past due and 90 days past due.

If you don't have a credit report reflecting your recent history, (six months) order your report. You will want to compare your credit history to your personal records.

Total the balances, and the payments due. We will get to the late charges in a minute, unless you are over the limit and have to make a large payment to avoid further charges in the next billing cycle.

On a new sheet, (I like legal pads because they give you line space and are long enough to get everything on one page.) list each account by length of time the account has been opened. List the amount due, and the balance. You don't have to add these totals, this is just to give you an idea of where you need to start when determining whether or not you need help to resolve the problems.

Just how bad is it:

When determining your payment schedule, put the oldest accounts first. The reasoning for this is a company you have dealt with for years may be more interested in working out an independent plan.

Reduce the highest debt first. Most people think they will get rid of the small debt first, because it is easier. This is where the parameters change. Initially make the minimum payments, even

Consumer Rights Concerning Debt Collection

Consumers can stop debt collectors from contacting them by writing the collector and requesting no further contact.

Within five days of initial contact, collectors must send consumers written notices stating amounts owed and to whom.

If a consumer has an attorney, the agency may contact only the attorney.

The agency may contact other third parties only to learn where the consumer is located.

Collectors cannot call a person at home before 8:00 a.m. or after 9:00 p.m.

Collectors are not allowed to tell anyone other than the consumer or attorney that the consumer owes money.

Collectors cannot say or imply that they will seize or garnish proper wages unless the creditor intends to do so.

For advice or to file a complaint, call the Federal Trade Commission. In Atlanta they can be reached at (404) 347-4836. You may want to leave a message if you call after hours. For a free brochure on debt collection, write to the FTC, Room 1000, 1718 Peachtree St., Atlanta, GA 30367-4101.

Source: Federal Trade Commission

without the interest just to keep the account current. If you go into a debt management program you are not going to get a reduction in interest, or stop late charges, for at least 90 days.

If you have ten accounts and you can not come up with the cash to bring all accounts current, write to your creditors and present a plan. Explain to them you don't want to file for bankruptcy or enter into a debt management plan. Inform your creditors of your current difficulty and explain to them the plan you have designed to pay your bills.

What if all the above fail? What if your debt is so deep you can't work out a plan to meet the high cost of having missed payments for several months? What if you have no personal resources to draw on? If you are already at a bare bones existence and need to find a way to increase cash flow by lowering expenditures, you need to put your pride aside and ask for help.

Asking for outside help:

Chapter 11, is federal bankruptcy law, with bankruptcy code being the informal name.

Bankruptcy is a legal proceeding that protects the debtor from legal action by creditors.

Research by the Federal Reserve indicates that household debt is at a record high relative to disposable income. Some analysts are concerned that this unprecedented level of debt might pose a risk to the financial health of American households. A high level of indebtedness among households could lead to increased household delinquencies and bankruptcies, which could threaten the health of lenders if loan losses are greater than anticipated. **(American Bankruptcy Institute)**

Before you consider bankruptcy as an option, understand that this is legal process, one that you should not go through without the assistance of an attorney. Chapter 7 gets rid of all debt except for some taxes, alimony and child support.

Even the simplest case requires miles of paper work. If you are already in trouble you don't want to purchase a do it yourself kit. Chances are it will be good money chasing after bad. If you can't manage a simple budget how can you file a hundred legal forms?

New bankruptcy laws are making it more difficult to file and put restrictions on the conditions of the action.

Bankruptcy should be the last resort, it is not a quick fix. The action stays on your credit report for ten years. I am not a financial expert, but it doesn't make sense to me to put money into a legal proceeding to clear debt.

Change the verbs from controlling to managing.
Another option is entering into a debt management program. This means hiring a third party to manage your debt and make payments to your creditors.

Shop around, know what you are getting and know what you are going to be required to pay for the program. Some programs like Consumer Credit Counseling Services (CCCS) are funded by voluntary contributions. Other programs charge a monthly fee for managing your debt plan. Read the small print, not only regarding the fee charged, but understand exactly how the program works.

A debt management program may be the best opportunity for you, but it doesn't come without a huge investment from you. To determine just exactly what that investment is you may want to talk to more than one counselor.

Don't be mislead by programs that claim to be non profit. A non profit may fuel the coffers of the CEOs while the associates that handle your financial plan are entry level phone operators. Debt management programs are just as competitive as their counterparts, home equity lenders, they make money off your debt, especially the interest.

When you decide to enter a program, you are making a commitment to pay your creditors. CCCS, because they have offices all over the country and deal with creditors from all sectors, may be able to get your payments reduced and interest lowered.

Understand though, the benefit of the program for reduced payments is not immediate. This is a long term commitment that requires your learning about every aspect of the plan.

Being enrolled in a debt management program is not a walk in the park. The length of the program will be determined by the amount of debt you owe.

Credit Repair:
This is a misleading term. There is no such thing as going into your credit report and repairing it. Don't be mislead by these offers. Often Consumer Credit Counseling agencies will make this claim.

Regardless of how you pay back debt, until you satisfy all your accounts or bring them current with payments, you can not repair your credit history.

Create a workable budget.

Learn to evaluate needs over wants. Getting on with life without being tied to your debt is a great feeling.

Once you become enrolled in a program you have to take full responsibility to monitor each monthly statement and make certain payments are posted. Your program will send you a contract and proposals for payment to your creditors. Once the proposals are accepted the payments begin. The counselors make every effort to work out a payment plan that will not be impossible for you to incorporate into your everyday cost of living.

Creditors can reject proposals and require a larger payment. Most of the programs have a small cushion to offset a new proposal by the creditor. However you may be asked to increase your deposit.

Not only are you relieved from the stress of dealing with overdue bills, and unwanted phone calls, but also the responsibility of writing the checks and mailing the payments.

Each creditor reports your payment history according to their criteria. If you are making a monthly payment and fulfilling the requirements of the program, your current status and payment history is not as important as the completion of the program.

Your program will send you a monthly statement, showing exactly where every penny of your deposit is applied. Check the statement carefully every month to track the payments and determine what lower interest is being charged.

If you find an error on the statement, call your program immediately.

When you begin setting up for a program it is very important to supply all information about every account. You can however make additional payments to help bring the debt down quicker.

Getting your house in order through a debt management plan is a second chance to recover your negative credit history.

Remember debt repayment plans will not include secured debt, like a mortgage or an automobile loan. The counselor spends a great deal of time on the initial interview to set up a plan for repayment and at the same time offers guidance towards all your financial obligations. As the old debt decreases, your ability to cover expenses and develop savings for the future will increase, along with the peace of mind that comes with being responsible.

Student Loans

Since 1966, MORE THAN 116 MILLION LOANS HAVE BEEN ISSUED UNDER THE Federal Family Education Loan Program, representing more than 343 BILLION IN FEDERAL STUDENT LOANS.

Cost of Attendance - Expected Family Contribution = Financial Need:

Financial aid is a combination of scholarships, grants, student loans and federal work-study programs. The student loan limit is determined by the other financial aid you receive and is meant to close the gap to cover all costs for an academic year in approved programs at accredited schools. Before you run to the nearest bank to apply for a student loan you need to understand the steps that lead to all financial aid including student loans. Completing a four-page form the Free Application for Federal Student Aid (FAFSA), is the first step in the financial process. The form should be completed in January of the senior year, or as early in the year of attendance as possible but cannot be filed before January 1, in the year of attendance.

The FAFSA provides information about you and your family's income that will be used to determine the expected family contribution for your education. The difference between your family contribution and the cost of attendance will determine your financial need.

The form is a lot like filling out loan papers for a mortgage. You will need your tax return (or a close estimate), W-2s, 1099s, and any other records of money earned including untaxed income, plus bank statements, mortgage documents, business records (including farm records if applicable), and all investment accounts. The formula used to determine your financial aid needs considers family income, accumulated savings, amount of taxes paid, family size, the age of the oldest parent and when that parent expects to retire, the number of children enrolled in college at the same time, and the student's own financial resources, like an education IRA or ESA or other income or inherited wealth. It is almost like a test when answering the questions; you have to answer all the questions. Estimate if you have to, then investigate to correct the answers later.

The full cost of tuition, books, room and board etc. are referred to by the government as Cost of Attendance. Check and double check the form, be sure to sign it. Also you might want to check with the schools you are interested in to see if they offer the FAFSA electronically. You will receive a Student Aid Report (SAR) in about four weeks,stating the expected family contribution. Schools will send you an award letter detailing the financial aid you are eligible for.

A renewal FAFSA should be sent each year, review the responses, make sure all information is correct and you will receive aid according to the award decided for each year until academic completion. Contact your school if you don't receive the renewal form by February 15th if you don't want to go through the initial process of filling out the FAFSA again.

Student Loans:

Federal Family Education Loan Program (FFELP) includes Federal Stafford loans Perkins Loans and PLUS loans (loans for parents). These are all long-term low interest loans for attendance at eligible schools.

Federal Direct Student Loan Program offers loans directly to the students through the schools. The lender then disburses the school's annual allotment and the school credits this to the students' financial aid account. Sallie Mae is the largest corporate partner in the Federal Family Education Loan Program (FFELP). Authorized by congress in 1965, this program allows one out of three families to obtain a share of almost $28 million dollars in funds each year. The program while designed to help American families is also a bargain for the American taxpayer. Costs of the program have dropped from 8.5 cents for every loan dollar outstanding in 1991 to 0.8 cents in 2000.

Student loans are good debt, very low interest, anxiety free, no collateral or credit check. There are two types of loans; Subsidized and unsubsidized awarded on the basis of financial need.

The following questions will determine a student's dependency status which is the main factor in deciding which loan will be made available.

- Was the student born before January 1980?
- Is the student an orphan or ward of the court?
- Is the student a Veteran of the U.S. Armed Forces?
- Is the student currently married?
- Will the student be working on a degree beyond a bachelor's degree in school year 2003-2004?
- Does the student have dependents (other than his or her spouse) that he or she supports?

If one or more of the above conditions apply, the student is an INDEPENDENT STUDENT.

If none of these conditions apply, the student is considered to be DEPENDENT and parental information is used to determine financial aid eligibility.

Both subsidized and unsubsidized loans are offered through the Stafford loan programs with the funds coming from a bank, credit union or other lenders participating in the program. Stafford loans can be obtained through two formats; one is the FFELP with the funds coming from a private lender such as a bank, credit union or other designated lenders. While the funds for the Direct Loan program come directly from the federal government. Both programs have identical eligibility requirements and limits of loans, but offer different repayment options. Financial need determines the subsidized loans and has no impact on unsubsidized loans; in fact you can receive both loans within an enrollment period. The federal government subsidizes the interest before repayment and during authorized periods of deferment.

Interest is charged on an unsubsidized loan from the time the loan is disbursed until it is paid in full. You can begin payments on the interest or you can have the interest capitalized. If you choose the capitalized option you will have to repay more because the interest will be added to the principal amount of your loan and additional interest will be based on the higher amount. Paying interest as it accumulates, you'll repay less in the long run.

Dependent undergraduate students can borrow up to $2,625.00 as first year students and $3,500.00 when you have completed your first year of study if you have at least one full year of study. If you have completed two full years of a program you can receive $5,500, if you meet the standard of having the remainder of your program <u>as a full academic year</u>.

An independent undergraduate student or a dependent student, whose parents can not get a PLUS loan, can get unsubsidized loans with higher annual amounts.

- First year students—$6,625 ($2,625 subsidized)
- Students having completed first year—$7,500 ($3,500 subsidized)
- Students having completed two years of study—$10,500 ($5,500 subsidized)
- Graduate students can borrow up to $18,500 ($8,500 subsidized) each academic year.

Combined outstanding debt from Stafford loans: $23,000 dependent undergraduate loan, $46,000 independent undergraduate loan ($23,000 subsidized) and a graduate or professional student can borrow $138,500 ($65,000 subsidized). This amount includes loans for undergraduate study. Be aware, your school can refuse to certify your loan application or certify the loan for less than the amount you are eligible for. This decision cannot be appealed to U.S. Department of Education.

Parent loans (PLUS Loans)

Taking out a loan to supplement your child's financial aid package is an opportunity for parents to get a lower interest loan than a private loan. Plus loans are simple interest loans and not compound interest loans like credit cards and some home equity loans. The variable interest rate is adjusted annually but will never exceed 9%. In fact, with the interest rate being lowered by the Federal Reserve to an all time low, PLUS loans are at all time low interest rates. The borrower is notified of interest rate changes (July 1), throughout the life of the loan.

The interest rate is calculated on the T-Bill rate plus 3.1% up to the 9% cap. Check with your lending institution to determine if they use the 52 week T-Bill or the 90 day T-Bill, it is just something you should know but in the long run will not have much effect on the interest in this time when low interest rules.

PLUS loans are restricted like student loans on the cost of attendance, expected family contribution and all other financial aid. If your student's cost of attendance is $8,000.00 and he or she has received $6,000.00, the PLUS loan will be approved for up to $2,000.00 and no more.

The loan funds will be disbursed to the school, probably in two installments. No installment can be greater than half the loan amount. The funds must be used to pay tuition, fees, room and board and other school charges. Fees up to 4% are charged for the loan in addition to the interest. Repayment begins 60 days after the final loan disbursement for the period of enrollment the money was borrowed. The interest accrues when the first disbursement is made and parents, unlike students as borrowers, will begin repayment for both principal and interest while the student is in school. Although parents will have to go through a credit check the credit requirements are very lenient for a PLUS loan compared to other credit.

These low cost loans have deferment opportunities and no pre-payment penalty. When the full cost of education, in any given enrollment year can not be covered by the financial aid available to a student, parents of dependent students can borrow enough money to meet the financial burden left from a financial aid package. PLUS loans can be obtained in the same manner as student loans, through FFELP or direct loans.

Consolidation Loans:

These loans make the repayment process easier but do involve a higher interest rate. There are some alternate programs for repayment that the student should consider if they are having trouble paying their loans. Lower payments based on income, graduated repayment during the first two years after graduation and extended repayment allows the borrower to extend the loan without consolidation. The increase in interest for each of these options is less than the total interest charged in consolidation.

When you consider the possibility of consolidating your loans it is good to consider the timing. Take advantage of the lower rates by consolidating loans for repayment to get the lower "in school" interest rate.

A consolidation loan combines several student (or parent) loans in one bigger loan from a single lender which is then used to pay off the balances on all the other loans from several lenders.

Consolidation loans often reduce the size of the monthly payment. Depending on the size of the new loan, the term of the loan can be extended from 12 to 30 years, however extending the term of the loan may increase the amount of interest.

The interest rate for a consolidation loan takes into considera-tion the weighted average of the interest rates on the current loans to be rounded up to the nearest 1/8 of a percent and capped at 8.25%. Regardless of the percentages the net savings is usually substantial when you consolidate. Graduate students may find it necessary to consolidate in order to qualify for a mortgage loan.

Currently the interest on Stafford and PLUS loans are at an all time low. If you are making payments on a Stafford loan in 2003 your repayment rate will be at 4.06%. The rate for those in school, in a grace period, or in deferment, is 3.46%, making this very good debt and hassle free.

Private Loans:

The amount borrowed will be determined by the lending institu-tion based on the your creditworthiness and your credit history. This money is not considered financial aid and it does not come through federal lenders. Private loans cost more than federal loans, but they can provide more money for education and may have more flexible repayment options, including deferred repayments. The student's level of study will help the lender determine the different type of loans to offer. There are no federal forms to fill out.

Payment Difficulties and Loan Forgiveness:

Repayment of student loans is like death and taxes: There may come a time when circumstances like the situations we talk about in earlier sections prevent you from paying your student loan. There is the possibility of a deferment or forbearance. If you are experienc-ing economic hardship, that is when the borrower is earning less than minimum wage or under the poverty line for a family of two. If the borrower has monthly payments on a federal loan or loans that are equal to or higher than 20% of the borrow-er's gross monthly income it is also considered economic hardship.

Under a deferment no payments are required and no interest accrues. Payments are postponed or reduced in forbearance, however interest continues to accrue and you are responsible to pay it. A Perkins loan can be canceled upon your death or a total and permanent disability. There is also a possibility the loan can be canceled based on the type of work the borrower does once he leaves school. By exchanging volunteer work or military service you can secure loan forgiveness that offers the ability to have the loan paid off. When you are in this situation, it is important to contact the school you intend to apply to, even if you had not filled out the form for student aid. If you should get into trouble meeting your loan obligations there are some recourses, however we want you to understand that this is a last resort, to be considered only when there are no other options. Subsidized loans will not accrue interest during the postponement of payments. On unsubsidized loans the borrower is responsible for interest.

When you don't pay the interest as it accrues it will be capitalized, increasing the amount of interest when you start repayment. Forbearance is a method where loan payments are reduced or postponed. Interest will accrue whether the loan is subsidized or unsubsidized and you will be charged interest and unpaid interest will be capitalized. Your consideration for forbearance includes being unable to make payment due to poor health or other unforeseen personal problems. You have to contact the Direct Loan Servicing Center (1-800-848-0979) to request either option if you have a Direct Stafford loan. Contact your lender or the agency that holds your FFELP Stafford loan.

Loan forgiveness is a term applied to a process where the federal government, through the military or national service organizations like AmeriCorps, Volunteers in Service to America (VISTA) or the Peace Corps, will pay the debt or part of the debt in exchange for a service commitment. To qualify you must be able to give a specific period of time to do volunteer work, teach or practice medicine in low income communities or sign up for service in the the National Guard or other uniformed services. The AmeriCorps program provides an award of $42,725 for one full-time term (1700 hours). If you have to leave the service for compelling reasons after you have fulfilled at least 15% of your commitment you still may be eligible for a prorated award. Another program that will forgive up to 15% of a loan is The National Defense Act. It is one thing to know that these programs exist but it is more important to pursue your student loans with the intent to fulfill the obligation.

Grants: Financial aid based on need that does not require repayment.

Nearly four and a half million students received Pell grants during the year 2002, totaling almost eleven billion dollars. Pell grant awards are made to students with an Expected Family Contribution of $4000 or less. Besides the regular grants many states are canceling up to $5,000 of a Stafford loan for teaching in low income schools, for five consecutive and complete school years.

Because of its eligibility criteria, the Pell Grant program serves primarily low-income students. Congress has continued to approve proposed increases for funding nevertheless the maximum grant level only covers 3/4 of the cost of higher education. The maximum award for the 2002-2003 award year is $4,000.00. Students enrolled in post baccalaureate teacher certification programs may be eligible for Pell grants. This grant is only given to borrowers that took out their first Stafford loan after October 1, 1998 and that have no outstanding balance on a previous loan.

The purpose of the Pell grant is to expand access to universities, and colleges for low-income students and provide the foundation of financial aid to which other aid, including federal work-study awards and student loans can be added.

The Pell grant depends on program funding at your school and you can only receive one grant in an award year. The grant you receive will not only depend on your estimated family contribution but also the cost of attendance for your school, if you are a full or part time student and a full academic year of attendance (or less). It is important for students to complete their education, however almost half of those who enter college never get a degree. To get the best for the dollars invested students must leave the college or university with a degree.

Federal Work Study program:

This program provides part time employment for the undergraduate student to help pay for the cost of education and participate in community service programs at the same time. The school may use part of the work study grant to develop and locate jobs for program participants.

Your total work study award depends on both your financial need and the funding level at the school. Your academic progress and class schedule plays a part in assigning hours as well as your award amount.

Wages in the program have to meet minimum wage standards but depending on the work you do could be higher. Wages are paid at an hourly rate, at least once a month. The Federal Work-Study program is considered one of the best ways to gain financial aid while gaining valuable experience in a chosen field and providing a service to the community.

Scholarships:

Billions of dollars in scholarships are available for merit in academics, athletics, and artistic talent. In general there is a scholarship for every need, both genders and cultural and ethnic groups. While scholarships are not limited to the 4.0 student, maintaining a high grade point average is crucial to renewing awards and securing new scholastic opportunities.

Once you have been admitted to a school inquire about the scholarships the school offers through the Admissions department. Several scholarships for superior academic development are made available to the high school seniors admitted for the next academic year. Alumni associations, sororities, fraternities, and individual departments offer substantial awards based on grade point average, class rank, and test scores.

The best way to find out about the scholarships available in your area as well as your school is to check with the Public Library. Request a list of scholarships being offered by local service organizations (Lions, Rotary, Elks, American etc.) from your school counselor. Both high school and alumni associations of the schools parents attended also offer scholarship opportunities. Corporate sponsors also provide scholarships in areas of business, science, education and sports. Under represented groups in many fields are sought actively to participate in corporate programs. The Miss America Pageant is the largest individual provider of scholarships giving over 40 million dollars of aid each year to pageant contestants that never reach the stage for the final Miss America competition in Atlantic City.

Title IX has opened many scholarship opportunities for the woman athlete since its inception over 25 years ago. Schools regardless of their size have active athletic programs and offer scholarships in sports like soccer, golf, tennis and gymnastics.

Two of the better known programs that offer assistance to ethnic groups are the Asian Pacific American Heritage Council (APHAC) and the United Negro College Fund (UNCF). The APHAC has established scholarships for studies in business, education, finance, law, law and public service. The UNCF an educational assistance program founded in 1944 provides financial support to 40 private historically black colleges and universities. One of the most provocative statements we saw in describing programs is the registered trademark of the UNCF-A Mind is a Terrible Thing to Waste.

Military options from high school to retirement:

The U.S. Armed forces offers many education programs both to pay for your education and repayment of student loans in exchange for a certain period of military service.

- **Montgomery GI Bill (MGIB):** Up to 36 months of educational benefits for a degree or certification program, apprenticeships, flight training and correspondence courses after release from active duty.
- **Top Up:** An amendment to the GI Bill that allows the VA to pay a benefit equal to the difference between the total cost of a college course and the other assistance from the military.
- **Maryland in Europe:** A consortium of five Maryland state institutions offering associate, bachelor's and master's degrees to the U.S. Military and their dependents overseas.
- **Tuition Assistance (TA):** Allows enlisted men to enroll in courses at accredited colleges, universities, junior colleges, high schools and vocational technical schools.
- **Student Loan Repayment Program (LRP):** Will pay back up to$65,000 dollars of qualified student loans when you enlist. Reservists can receive up to $20,000.00. Private alternative loans or defaulted loans will not qualify.
- **Reserve Officers Training Corps (ROTC):** A program that provides education training in exchange for a specific period of service when your degree is completed.
- **National Guard and Reserves** also offer educational programs to high school seniors that take their basic training before the beginning of their senior year and complete 2 years of service. Be sure to contact both active duty and reserve recruiters to find all the options available.

Life Experience Credits:

Another way to put to use what you already have learned is credit for life experiences. Academic credit for knowledge gained in the real world. This is a process that allows students to identify and organize their skills learned through experience and to connect their experience to academic knowledge. Check with your college or program to see how much credit can be earned for life experiences. This process begins with demonstrating prior learning to outside evaluators and professionals in the community.

Life experience credits are also earned through skills and knowledge attained through work experience, formalized or special training, military service, attendance at workshops, conferences and seminars. Licenses, certifications, authored papers or books and community service must directly relate to one or more course curriculum in the degree program you select.

College Level Examination Program (CLEP):

CLEP is a solution crafted by college and university faculty to present exams in dozens of subjects to gain college credit without taking the course. Over 600 professors nationwide create and set the standards for this program to test students on material they have mastered and can demonstrate proficiency through testing on course materials. Check the college you wish to attend regarding the policies on CLEP at their school. There are some schools that offer CLEP for graduate students. This involves taking the final exam and getting a grade of at least 85% to get credit for the course.

Financial aid takes a great deal of responsibility to fulfill the promise you make when you accept aid. One thing to remember is the competition gets stiffer every year for all types of financial aid.

INVESTMENT ACCOUNTS AND OTHER EDUCATIONAL SAVINGS PLANS:

Long headings and acronyms can be very annoying. None of the acronyms we have used thus far are nearly as confusing as the Uniform Transfers to Minors Act (UTMA) *(formerly the Uniform Gifts to Minors Act)*. The essential aspects of both acts are the same but the new law is more flexible. The District of Columbia, Vermont and South Carolina are the only areas that haven't established the Uniform Transfers to Minors Act. The new act allows you to expand the types of property you can transfer to a minor, and also provides for other types of transfers besides gifts. Read the fine print of the law in your state because even though it is called the Uniform Act, laws are similar but not identical.

Custodial accounts for college planning.

The best use of custodial accounts are in situations where you want to make a financial gift to a son, daughter or grandchild and the gift isn't focused on the tax benefits. When the dollar amount is modest this is a good vehicle for giving the child a taste of ownership while watching savings grow. It is one way leave a gift to your beneficiaries without bearing a large estate tax. Consider giving the estate in annual amounts too small to be subject to gift tax. You can transfer $300,000 over 15 years without paying any gift tax and the minor also gets the benefit of the earnings accrued over the fifteen years.

These accounts were established to give parents and grandparents the ability to open mutual fund accounts because minors cannot own mutual funds outright. The accounts are considered custodial accounts because while the account is opened in the minor's name and under the minor's social security number, a custodian is responsible for managing the assets until the child reaches the age of majority. The UTMA allows almost any asset to be gifted to minors and is not restricted to cash, mutual funds, securities and insurance policies. There is no limit to the contributions and anyone can contribute. Gifts over $10,000 per year ($20,000) from married couples filing jointly are allowed but may be subject to federal gift taxes.

The custodian can withdraw funds from the account for the child's benefit, for an education, new car or whatever the child may need. Read over the prospectus very carefully and get advice if you are not sure of what you are doing before you invest or send money to open the account.

Only the beneficiary has the right to the funds, and the custodian manages for the benefit of the minor. The child takes ownership of the property as soon as it is transferred to the account, and not when the account terminates. A gift to this account can not be withdrawn for any purpose by the giver, and income generated by assets in the account is the child's income. The adult custodian can be taxed on the income if the account is abused.

Income on the accounts is reported under the child's social security, as the tax obligation for minors is much lower than for adults. For a child under fourteen, the first seven hundred dollars of unearned income is tax-free and earnings from seven hundred to fourteen hundred are taxed at the children's income tax rate. All earnings over fourteen hundred dollars are taxed at the adult rate. Check with your accountant or financial advisor for exact details regarding the tax obligations through all stages of the account until the minor reaches the age of majority and takes control of the account. Once the minor reaches the age of majority, (18 or 21 depending on the state of residence), the custodian loses all control over the account.

Other Options for Educational Savings Plans:

There is a new option for long term savings to pay for college tuition. The limited Education IRA is a thing of the past replaced by a new program called Coverdell Education Savings Accounts (ESA).The account can be opened at any bank or IRS approved savings entity.

Income limits have been increased allowing couples with adjusted gross incomes of $190,000 or less to contribute the maximum and couples earning between $190,000 and $220,000 can save smaller amounts. This money can be used to pay for primary and secondary school education costs such as public school uniforms, private school tuition, educational computer technology or equipment, academic tutoring, transportation and other education related expenses. The cost of room and board can be either the school posted room and board or $2,500 each year for a student living off campus. The contribution is not deductible on your tax return but can be used tax free under certain conditions, like the above mentioned uses. Parents, grandparents, family members and friends can contribute to a child's account up to the $2,000 limit per tax year.

The terms of the ESA are much more compatible with education needs than the old Education IRA. The child can contribute to his own ESA and does not need to be enrolled for a minimum number of semesters to take a tax free withdrawal. Amounts unused by the beneficiary of an ESA must be withdrawn when the beneficiary turns 30.

Income on the account is reported under the child's Social Security number because the child's income tax rate is lower than adults and gives the child the experience of owning a mutual fund with tax savings. It is important to get into the right funds under proper management or you can increase the tax obligations.

Conclusion:

Learning to make the most of what we have is usually a lesson we are taught early in life. Adding to that premise we want you to keep as much as you can of your hard earned salaries to attain the lifestyle you find the best for your family.

Be aggressive in determining your needs and don't fall victim to the advice of anyone, family member, friend or creditor. It is your money, spend wisely, save and plan for the future according to your needs and plans.

Don't be intimidated by creditors or by circumstances.

Always keep in mind that life situations can occur without warning that will change every aspect of your life, including your finances. Have a safety cushion to fall back on.

Lifestyle changes often require planning, keeping good financial records will allow you the insight to gauge future needs.

Don't jump into deals on the spur of the moment that could affect your personal portfolio for years to come.

Before you apply for a personal loan, lease a car, refinance your mortgage or get a home equity loan, investigate all the options. Know what you have and what you can lose.

Take time to read the glossary terms, study applications and contracts. Don't be a victim of small print fallout.

Don't minimize the value of a safety cushion and put it off until it will be easier to do. You can't afford to risk the loss of health insurance and other necessities in the event of an unexpected event that takes your income away.

When you can afford to invest, go slowly, and again investigate all the options, fees and limitations.

Never underestimate the importance of your personal papers. Your wishes can not be carried out if they are not made known through a will and insurance policies.

When you are at the end of the rope financially, don't let embarrassment keep you from getting help. Carefully assess what you have and select a debt management program.

Aside from your other financial goals consider working on getting the lowest interest and the fewest points on your next mortgage.

Do everything you can to protect your family. Keeping good records, organizing personal papers and listing your debt and savings will help you plan for the future. Devise a plan then stick to it.

Never give up too much when getting a line of credit or home equity loan, look to the future and deal from strength and not weakness.

In The Back of the Book
– Terms and Definitions

Often the questions we ask have more of an impact on a situation than the answers we give. For instance, when you are being interviewed for a position, if the only questions you ask are about the benefits, you may not get past the first interview. If you don't ask about the company's mission you can not be competitive with other applicants. Sick days, vacation days and lunch breaks are important, but not nearly as important as the job description you will be expected to fill. The smart applicant finds out as much as she can before the interview.

When it comes to applying for credit in any form, but especially credit cards and home equity loans, you need to do more than let your fingers do the walking. The questions you ask (or don't ask) will impact every aspect of the process. Learn the terms of the trade. Be aggressive.

Consumer literacy is an important quality to acquire whether you are correcting information on a credit report, negotiating the best terms and interest rates for a loan or learning to resolve disputes with your bank or creditors. In fact, learning to understand many of the glossary terms will give you the ability to make much better credit decisions.

The appendix material gives you an up front look at the forms, practices and procedures of many of the businesses and agencies you will deal with. Most of us are familiar with federal agency acronyms, like FAA, FCC and IRS. However very few of us have any idea of how much protection under the law we have through the Federal Trade Commission. Probably the two most important pieces of legislation for the American consumer are The Federal Credit Reporting Act and the Truth in Lending Act. Many of us aren't connected to the internet or if we are, we don't have the expertise to search out and find the volumes of information offered www.ftc.gov.

Using the information in the glossary and the appendix will give you a head start at becoming consumer smart. Once you learn about the laws and regulations covering the credit card and mortgage industry, you will make much better choices and get more for your money in the market place.

Accelerated payment:
Scheduled payment plus additional monthly payment. Leads to a quicker payoff of debt and less interest paid over the life of the loan.

Acceleration clause:
A provision in a mortgage or equity loan that gives the lender the right to demand payment of the entire principal balance if a monthly payment is missed.

Acceptance:
An offeree's consent to enter into a contract and be bound by the terms of the offer.

Account condition:
The state of the account, current, past due, etc., but it does not reflect your actual payment history. In other words increased payments even double payments will not reflect on your status when you miss a payment.

Accounts in good standing:
Credit items that are positive and help your creditworthiness.

Account monitoring:
Once lenders make a yes decision, they might want to review your credit report on a regular basis as they continue to manage their financial risk. This monitoring scans credit reports for certain risk characteristics as defined by the lender. Federal laws specifically permits lenders to monitor their accounts. When you signed your credit application, you gave the lender permission to access your credit report from time to time.

Acquisition fee:
Refers to price to purchase another company or property.

Additional monthly payment:

The amount of your extra payment per month. This amount is in addition to your minimum required payment and will reduce your principal balance more quickly.

Additional principal payment:

A payment by a borrower of more than the scheduled principal amount due in order to reduce the remaining balance on the loan.

Adjusted basis:

The original cost of a property plus the value of any capital expenditures for improvements to the property minus any depreciation taken.

Adjustment:

The percentage of debt to be repaid to credit grantors in a Chapter 13 bankruptcy.

Adjustment Interval:

On an adjustable rate mortgage the time between changes in the interest rate and or monthly periods, one, three or five years depending on the index.

Adjustable rate mortgage:

A mortgage where the interest rate is liable to change over the term of the loan.

Adverse Action Notice:

This is a disclosure requirement that applies to new applicants for insurance as well as current policy holders. When a decision is made to deny insurance, increase rates, or terminate a policy, if it is based solely or partly on information in a consumer report, a notice of the adverse action must be provided to the consumer. (Section 615 (a) The Fair Credit Reporting Act)

Affordability analysis:

A detailed analysis of your ability to afford the purchase of a home. This analysis takes into consideration your income, liabilities, and available funds, along with the type of mortgage you plan to use, the area where you want to purchase a home, and the closing costs you might expect to pay.

Affinity card:
A card offered jointly by two organizations. One is a credit card issuer and the other is a professional organization, special interest group or other non-bank company.

Aid Package:
A combination of scholarships, grants, and work study contracts.

Amenity:
A feature of real property that enhances its attractiveness and increases the occupant's or user's satisfaction although the feature is not essential.

Amortization:
The process of fully paying off your debt by installments of principal and earned interest over a fixed time.

Amount Past Due:
Current amount delinquent on loan.

Annual Fee:
Once a year cost of owning a credit card.

Annual income:
Yearly income. For married couples this is your total combined yearly income, after taxes for spending purposes, and the gross for entitlement and tax purposes.

Annual interest rate:
Amount of interest you will pay over one year, expressed as a percentage of your balance. Maximum interest rate is 20 percent.

Annual Percentage Rate (APR):
A measure of how much interest will cost, expressed as an annul percentage. Interest rate reflecting the cost of mortgage is a yearly rate.

Annual Rate Of Return:
Pretax rate of return on the amount earned on savings and investments. For example, the long term rate of return for investments in the stocks that make up the S&P 500 is about 11%. A savings account earns 2 to 5%.

Appraisal:
An expert judgement or estimate of the quality or value of real estate, made by an appraiser, as of a given date.

Application Fee:
Fee paid upon application that includes an appraisal and credit report.

Asset:
Anything owned by an individual that has cash value. This includes property, goods, savings or investments.

Association code:
Describes the consumer's relationship to an account (primary responsibility, authorized users)

Assumption:
The agreement between buyer and seller where the buyer takes over the payments on an existing mortgage from the seller. Assuming a loan can usually save the buyer money since this is an existing mortgage debt, unlike a new mortgage where closing cost and new, probably high, market rate charges will apply.

Authorized user:
Person permitted by credit cardholder to charge goods and services on the cardholder's account. The card holder is responsible for charges made by an authorized user.

Average daily balance:
The average daily balance is a method used to calculate finance charges on an account. It is calculated by adding the outstanding balance on each day in the billing period, and dividing that total by the number of days in the billing period. The calculations include new purchases and payments. The daily interest rate is then applied to the daily balance to calculate the finance charge.

B or C loans:
Loans that reflect less than the best possible interest rate, terms and conditions. Consumers with negative or derogatory credit may be offered a B or C loan with a higher interest rate and fees.

Bad debt:
A debt the lender has determined the borrower is not going to pay.

Balance:
Total amount owed on an account or mortgage or the amount in your savings or checking account.

Balance transfer:
Moving a balance from one account to another. In the case of a credit account, the balance (debt) is moved from one credit card to another.

Balloon loan:
Short term fixed-rate loan which involves small payments for a certain period of time and one large payment for the remaining amount of the principal at a time specified in the contract.

Bankruptcy:
When a debtor is legally declared unable to pay debts as they become due.

Bankruptcy Code:
Federal laws governing the conditions and procedures under which individuals and businesses that are unable to repay their debts can seek relief.

Base Federal Stafford Loan amount:
The base amount of a student's eligibility for a loan equaling the loan limit applicable to a dependent undergraduate student.

Bequest:
Assets that are transferred to an heir through a will. This gift may include money as well as personal property to a specific person or persons, and organizations.

Better Business Bureau:

A voluntary, non profit group established by businesses to improve the code of business practice and to define fair standards and ethics in business. The Better Business Bureau is neither a government agency or consumer group.

Big Three:

The Consumer Reporting Agencies (CRA's) that govern all credit reports.

Equifax
P.O. Box 74021
Atlanta, GA 30374
(800) 685-1111

Experian
P.O. Box 2104
Allen, TX 75013
(888) 397-3742

Trans Union:
P.O. Box 1000
Chester, PA 19022
(800) 916 8800

Billing cycle:

Number of days between bills, usually 25 days.

Blanket Mortgage:

A mortgage on at least two pieces of real estate as security for the same mortgage.

Borrower-specific deferment:

The federal requirement for deferment applied to all of a borrower's loans, rather than to each separate loan.

Broker:

An individual in the business of assisting in arranging funding or negotiating contracts for a client without lending the money for a fee (commission).

Budget:

Records used to measure expenses against income to determine financial standing.

Buy Down:
Subsidized mortgage by the lender or home builder with lower interest rates the first few years of the loan.

Campus based aid:
Financial aid programs administered by a university. The federal government provides universities with a fixed annual allocation that is awarded by the financial aid administrator to deserving students.

Caps (Interest):
Consumer safeguards which limit the amount of the interest rate on an adjustable rate mortgage.

Capacity:
This is the combination of your income stability, employment history, amount in savings, and most importantly monthly debt payments compared to your income.

Cash advances:
Cash withdrawn on your credit card at a bank office or ATM. Cash advances usually carry fees and a higher APR than other charges.

Certificate of Eligibility:
Document of entitlement given to veterans for guaranteed loans on homes, businesses and mobile homes.

Certificate of Title:
Statement by provided by an abstract company, title company, or attorney stating that the title of estate is legally held by the current owner.

Certificate of Veteran Status:
Document given to veterans or reservists who have served 90 days of continuous active duty, including training time. Present DD214 to the local VA office with request for certificate of veteran status.

Closing costs and Closing:

Fees by the borrowers or dwellers during the closing of the mortgage loan, such as an origination fee, discount points, attorney's fees, title insurance, survey and any items which were prepaid, such as taxes and insurance escrow payments.

Charge off:

Action of transferring accounts deemed un-collectible to a category such as bad debt or loss. Such accounts will usually continue to be pursued by collectors, but are no longer considered part of a company's receivable or profit picture.

Collection agency:

Business service employed to collect creditors' unpaid or past due accounts. Collection agencies are compensated by a percentage of amount collected.

Collateral:

An asset that guarantees repayment of a loan at the risk of losing the asset if loan is not repaid according to the terms of the contract.

Co-maker:

Co-maker is legally responsible to repay the charges in the joint account agreement if the other person defaults.

Combined Loan to Value:

Relationship between the unpaid principal balances of all the mortgages on a property and the property's appraised value.

Compensating Factors:

Examination of a borrower's creditors, strengths and weaknesses. Such as late payments that can be compensated by cash reserves.

Consumer Credit information:

Credit report that includes the account payment history of your credit relationships for seven years and public record history for ten years.

Consumer Credit Counseling Services (CCCS):
A national non profit debt management organization with 600 offices.

Consolidation loan:
Loan that pays off all your existing debt, preferably at a lower average interest rate.

Conventional Loan:
Mortgage not insured by FHA or guaranteed by the VA

Consumer Reporting Agencies:
Companies that buy and sell information regarding your financial history including how you pay your bills, criminal history and if you have filed for bankruptcy or have been sued.

Credit Bureau:
An agency that gathers information about a consumer's credit relationships and provides creditors with credit reports and scores on consumers.

Credit Enhancement:
Method of reducing credit risk by requiring collateral including Letters of credit, mortgage insurance and other agreements to provide an entity with some assurance it will be compensated to some degree in the event of a financial loss.

Credit File:
Statements, credit relationships, credit history and payment patterns.

Credit History:
On time payments of mortgage, credit cards and any debts reported to CRAs.

Credit Investigation:
Investigation to verify credit report information disputed by a consumer.

Credit Report:
Information regarding a consumer's identity, credit relationships, court actions, consumer statements and previous inquiries into that file.

Credit Repair:
Claim to fix credit problems and repair bad credit reports.

Credit Score:
Computer generated number based on a statistical model that reflects your credit risk level. Higher numbers indicate lower risk.

Creditworthiness:
Lender's assertion of the ability to pay back a debt before issuing credit. This process includes determining your ability to pay back the credit card debt or loan through three areas of your credit history, capacity, collateral and credit.

Debt security:
An arrangement where the issuing company generally agrees to repay the principal amount borrowed and make interest payments according to an agreed schedule.

Debt to Income Ratio:
Ratio, expressed as a percentage, results when a borrower's monthly payment obligation on long term debts is divided by gross monthly income.

Decedent:
A person who has died.

Default:
Failure of a debtor to make loan repayments as agreed to in a loan contract.

Deferred interest:
When a mortgage is written with a monthly payment that is less than required to satisfy the note, the unpaid interest is deferred by adding it to the loan balance.

Delinquent / Derogatory accounts:
Accounts classified according to the time past due. Common classifications are 30,60, 90 and 120 days past due. Can also include accounts that have been charged off, gone to collectors, liens, bankruptcies or court judgment.

Discharged:
Debt a court declares no longer needs to be repaid due to bankruptcy. Alimony, child support, liability for willful and malicious conduct and certain student loans cannot be discharged.

Discount Points:
A fee that lenders charge to lower interest rate on a mortgage. One point equals one percent of the loan amount.

Earnest Money Deposit:
Deposit made by potential home buyer to show that he or she is serious about buying the house.

Economic Hardship:
This applies to repayment of student loans when a borrower is working full time but is not earning greater than the minimum wage or meeting the poverty line for a family of two. It is considered a hardship when monthly payments on a federal loan are equal to or greater than 20% of the borrower's monthly income.

Economic Index:
Represents a consolidated average of a major economic component such as wholesale prices, housing starts or inflation that is used to measure economic health.

Economic Indicator:
Key statistics of the economy that reveal the direction of the economy, for example, the unemployment rate and the inflation rate.

Education IRA:
This is a tax deferred savings and investment account for education expenses with a maximum contribution of $500 per year for children under 18. IRA contributions are not tax deductible. The funds must be used for college or graduate tuition, room, board or books by the time the student is 30.

Effective Administration of Guaranteed Loans for Education (EAGLE):
Sallie Mae operating system that tracks all of the Federal Family Loan Program origination and guarantee activities administered on behalf of customers.

Effective Gross Income:
Normal annual income including overtime that is regular or guaranteed. The income may be from more than one source. Salary is generally the principal source, but other income may qualify if it is significant and stable.

Effective Interest Rate:
Cost of credit on a yearly basis expressed as a percentage. Includes up front costs paid to obtain loan, usually a higher amount than the interest rate stipulated in the mortgage.

End User:
Person or company who is ultimate recipient of information. Sometimes information passes through a number of different processes before reaching the end user.

Escrow:
Money (or documents) deposited with a third party to be delivered upon the fulfillment of a condition.

Estate:
Ownership of an individual in real property. Sum total of all the real property and personal property owned by an individual at the time of death. All assets owned by an individual at death to be distributed according to a will or a court ruling if there is no will.

Equal Credit Opportunity:
If you can prove discrimination by a creditor you may sue for actual damages plus punitive damages up to $10,000 plus court costs and attorney's fees.

Examination of Title:
Report on the title from public records or an abstract of the title.

Executor:
Person appointed by the testator, the person who has made the will, one who has died leaving a valid will to carry out the directions and requests in his will after his death.

Fair Credit Billing Act (FCBA):
Federal law providing specific error resolution procedures to protect credit card customers from making payments on inaccurate billings.

Fair Credit and Charge Disclosure Act:
Part of the Truth in Lending Act requiring the disclosure of the costs involved in credit card plans that are offered by mail, telephone or applications distributed to the general public.

Fair Market Value:
Highest price a buyer is willing to - but not compelled to pay, would pay, and the lowest a seller willing but not compelled to sell would accept.

Fannie Mae / Federal National Mortgage Association (FNMA):
A tax paying corporation created by Congress to purchase and sell conventional residential mortgages as well as those insured by the FHA or guaranteed by the VA. Fanny Mae provides money at a more affordable rate than many other mortgage institutions.

Federal Family Loan Education Program (FFLEP):
Loans funded by private lenders, guaranteed by guarantors, and reinsured by the federal government.

Federal Housing Administration (FHA):
Agency of U.S. Department of Housing and Urban Development (HUD) main activity is insuring of residential mortgage loans made by private lenders. The FHA sets standards for construction and underwriting but does not lend money.

Federal Loans:
Loans guaranteed by the U.S. government.

Federal Perkins Loan:
Long term low interest loans to students attending post second-ary school.

Federal Interest Subsidy:
Assistance given by the federal government in which they pay the interest on student loans while the student is in school before loan repayment begins.

Federal Methodology (FM):
The need analysis formula mandated by federal law to determine a family contribution.

Federal Trade Commission (FTC)
Federal agency which administers and enforces rules to prevent unfair business practices.

FHA Co Insured Mortgage
Mortgage insured by the Federal Housing Administration and the originating lender to share the risk of loss in the event of the mortgagor's default.

FHA Mortgage Insurance:
Requires a fee up to 2.25 percent of the loan amount paid at the closing to insure the loan. FHA mortgage insurance requires an annual fee of up to 0.5 percent of the current loan amount, paid in monthly installments. The lower the down payment, the more years the fee must be paid.

FICO Score:
Credit score developed by Fair Isaac & Company to determine the likelihood that credit users will pay their bills.

Fixed Rate:
Annual percentage interest rate that does not change during the term of the loan.

Flood Insurance:
Insurance that compensates for physical property damage resulting from floods. It is required on properties located in flood plains, federally designated flood areas.

Forbearance:

Lender's postponement of legal action on a delinquent loan, when a borrower makes satisfactory arrangements to bring the overdue payments to date.

Foreclosure:

When a debtor fails to meet his obligations to pay back a loan, the lender can take back possession of any property (such as a house) used to secure repayment for the loan. Foreclosure is the legal action to take possession of the property.

Freddie Mac:

The Federal Home Loan Mortgage Corporation purchases conventional loans from Savings and Loan Corporations providing a secondary market.

Free Application for Federal Student Aid (FAFSA):

A form designed to determine your eligibility for financial aid and should be completed as early as possible in the year you decide to attend college.

General Bequest:

Allows the executor of a will to honor the bequest from any available source and does not have to take it from a designated fund.

Good Faith Estimate:

Written estimate of closing costs which a lender must provide within three days of submission your application.

Grace Period:

A period of time during which a loan payment may be paid after the due date without incurring a late payment.

High Risk:

Consumers with delinquencies, bankruptcies, charge-offs or public record items on their credit report. These are indications to lenders that a consumer has been an irresponsible user of credit and will likely be so in the future. High risk consumers may only be able to get credit with very high interest rates, if at all.

Holographic Will:

A will written entirely in the handwriting of the testator. Most states do not accept handwritten wills. The states that do have very strict rules. It is important to understand those rules relating to the necessity of a bond and an executor.

Home equity loan:

Fixed or adjustable rate loan obtained for a variety of purposes, secured by the equity in your home. Interest paid is usually deductible.

Home Equity Closing Costs:

Any costs other than interest added to the home equity loan. Costs can include any appraisal fees, points paid or other miscellaneous fees. Costs can be paid up front or added to the loan balance.

Home Equity Interest Rate:

Annual percentage rate for the home equity loan.

Home equity line of credit

Loan providing ability to borrow funds at the time and in the amount you choose up to maximum credit limit for which you have qualified. Repayment is secured by the equity in your property. Simple interest, payments on the outstanding balance is usually tax deductible when used for home improvements.

Income tax rate

Your federal state and local income tax rates combined. Your income tax rate is important in determining the amount you can save if you use a home equity loan to consolidate your debt.

Identity Theft:

When a consumer's financial information is obtained illegally and used for unauthorized purchases and transactions with credit cards or funds from savings and checking accounts.

Index:
Number indicating a change in quantity, as of prices, relative to the magnitude at some specified point usually taken as 100. Common indexes include the Cost of Funds for the Eleventh Federal District of Banks or the average rate of a one year Government Treasury Security.

Inheritance Tax:
A tax imposed on one that has inherited something. The recipient pays this tax.

Inquiry:
An inquiry is when you have applied for credit, which gives the lender permission to pull your credit report.

Installment Debt:
This option is less available and has been replaced by revolving debt. Credit accounts in which the debt is divided into amounts to be paid successively at specified intervals until the debt is paid off.

Impound:
That portion of a borrower's monthly payments held by the lender or service to pay for taxes, hazard insurance, mortgage insurance and other items as they come due.

Interest Rates:
The percent per unit of time, of the total sum borrowed that is charged by a bank or financial institution for the use of their money.

Intestate:
Dying without a will. Distribution of the decedent's estate will be overseen by a probate court.

Investigative Consumer Reports:
Reports ordered by a prospective employer for sensitive jobs where background checks and security clearances are necessary. An investigative consumer report might contain information obtained from a credit report, but it is more comprehensive than a credit report. It contains subjective material on an individual's character, habits and mode of living, obtained through interviewing the associates and neighbors of the person being investigated.

Investment Rate of Return:
Amount you expect to earn on your investments. This is the return that you would make if you were to invest your down payment, security deposit or closing costs instead of using it in your purchase or lease of an auto or purchase of a home.

Involuntary Bankruptcy:
A petition filed by certain credit grantors instead of by the individual or business to have a debtor judged bankrupt, if the bankruptcy is granted it is known as an involuntary bankruptcy.

Item Specific Statement:
The right to offer an explanation about a particular account or public record item to be posted on your credit report.

Judgment Granted:
Final determination issued by a court for the rights of parties involved in a lawsuit.

Lien:
Legal document used to create security interest in another's property. A lien is often given as a security for the payment of a debt. A lien can also be placed against a consumer for failure to pay the city, county, state or federal government money that is owed.

Lien Waiver:
Document that releases a consumer (homeowner) from any further obligation for payment of debt once it has been paid in full. Lien waivers are used by homeowners who hire a contractor to provide work and material to prevent any subcontractors or supplier of material from filing a lien against the homeowner for non-payment.

Line of Credit:
Amount of credit offered that is secured against an asset such as your home or other real estate.

Living Will:
A document that names someone to make healthcare decisions for you if you develop a condition that makes it impossible for you to speak for yourself and makes clear in the form of written instructions what medical treatment you would want if you can no longer speak for yourself.

Loan Origination Rate:
Percentage the lending institution charges to cover some of its processing costs in making a loan in addition to the interest it will earn.

Loan to Value Ratio:
Relationship between amount of mortgage loan and the appraised value of the property expressed as a percentage.

Margin:
Amount, usually a percentage, added to the index to determine the interest rate for adjustable rate mortgages.

Market Value:
Worth in the market place. Market value can change based on supply and demand.

Medium High Risk:
Delinquencies, charge-offs, or public record items, but not as many incidents as high risk. Still likely to pay high interest rates.

Medium Low Risk:
Responsible credit behavior, but most likely to have one or two delinquencies on credit report.

Montgomery GI Bill (MGIB):
Cash incentive to encourage military service that provides up to 36 months of educational benefits to eligible veterans for college, business, technical or avocation courses and extends to correspondence courses, apprenticeship training and flight school.

Monthly PMI:

Monthly cost of Private Mortgage Insurance (PMI) for home loans secured with less than 20% down. PMI is commonly estimated at 5 per cent of your loan balance each year. Monthly PMI is calculated by multiplying your starting loan balance by your PMI percent and dividing by 12. When your equity exceeds 20 per cent of the original purchase price, your PMI payment should drop to zero. However, you should contact your lender when this occurs, as it may not be removed automatically.

Mortgage:

Written agreement to repay a loan. The agreement is secured by a mortgage, serves as proof of an indebtedness, and states the manner in which it shall be paid. The note states the actual amount of the debt a mortgage secures.

Negative Amortization:

Occurs when monthly payments are not large enough to pay all the interest due on the loan and unpaid interest is added to the unpaid balance of the loan. The danger in negative amortization is the home buyer ends up owing more than the original amount of the loan.

Net Home Price:

Selling price of a home after subtracting sales commissions.

Net House Payment:

House payment minus value of tax deduction and principal.

Non Assumption Clause:

Statement in the contract forbidding the assumption of the mortgage without the prior approval of the lender.

Notice of Results:

If you've requested an investigation of information on your credit report, you're entitled to receive a notice of results if your information was updated or deleted. You may request the credit bureau to send the corrected information in your credit history to credit grantors and employers who reviewed your information.

Office of Thrift Supervision:

The regulatory and supervisory agency for federally chartered savings institutions. Formally know as Federal Home Loan Bank Board.

Opt Out:

This is a number provided to remove your name and address from the credit bureau lists for unsolicited credit and insurance. This service is good for two years. For permanent removal from the lists you must request a form from the Credit Reporting Agencies. The opt out number is. 1-888-567-8688.

Parent Loans (PLUS):

Loans provided by private lenders or through the government to supplement the aid package of dependent children. Payments begin 60 days after the funds are fully disbursed with a repayment schedule up to ten years.

Payday Loan:

Short-term loan (14 days) secured with post dated check.

Payment Status:

Reflects history of payments on an account, including delinquencies or late payments occurring during the previous seven years (current account, delinquent 30 days, current was 60 days past due, redeemed repossession, charge off not paying etc.).

Pell Grant:

A federal grant for undergraduate education from the federal government that does not have to be paid back.

Permissible Purposes:

Circumstances under which a third party may obtain a consumer credit report. Permissible Purpose includes credit transactions, employment purpose, insurance underwriting, governmental financial responsibility laws, court orders, and subpoenas on written instructions of the consumer.

Personal Information:

Personal information section on your credit report that includes your name (and any name variations), driver's license number, social security number, date and year of birth, spouse's name employers, personal phone numbers and information about your residence. The consumer, creditors or other sources, report this information.

Personal statement:

Personal statement that will appear at the beginning of your credit report offering a general explanation about information on your report.

Petition:

When a consumer files bankruptcy, but a judge has not yet ruled it can proceed, the process is known as a bankruptcy petition.

Principal, Interest, Tax and Insurance (PITI):

Percent of your annual income the financial institution will allow you to use for your Principal, interest, tax and insurance payment for your home. The customary amount of your income to be used for PITI is 28 per cent, but can vary among lenders. This number is very important.

Point Scoring:

Assignment of values for characteristics identified as indicators of a person's credit worthiness. Point scoring is based on the same evaluation process used by a credit grantor in the analysis of an applicant's application.

Pre Payment:

Privilege in mortgage lending allowing the borrower to make payment in advance of due date.

Pre-Payment Penalty:

Charges imposed by lenders for paying a loan off earlier than the original pay off date to compensate for lost interest.

Pre-Payment Mortgage:
Mortgage type posing a prepayment penalty for repaying the loan or a substantial (20 percent or original value) portion of it within a certain period.

Predatory Lending:
Mortgages made to a borrower when the lender knows the borrower does not have the income to repay the loan. These lenders repeatedly refinance the loan charging high fees and points each time. The predatory lender also packs credit insurance into the loan. This practice is called stripping, and could result in the consumer losing their property.

Predictive Variables:
Items in the formula or factors of a credit scoring model.

Principal:
Amount of debt, not including interest.

Private Mortgage Insurance (PMI):
In the event you do not have a 20 per cent down payment, lenders will allow a smaller down payment, as low as five percent in some cases. With the smaller down payment, however, banks are usually required to carry private mortgage insurance. Private Mortgage Insurance will usually be at an initial premium payment and may require an additional monthly fee depending on your loan's structure.

Public Record Data:
Events like bankruptcies, foreclosures, repossessions, property and tax liens are part of courthouse records and could have a severe impact on your creditworthiness.

Qualifying Income:
Minimum monthly income range required to qualify for a loan payment.

Qualifying Ratios:
Comparisons of a borrower's debts and gross monthly income.

Quitclaim:

A deed that transfers whatever interest or title a grantor may have, without warranty. This document is primarily used to transfer ownership of real property from owner to buyer. The deed must be filed with the county in your state, transferring the property from the owner to the buyer.

Rate Cap:

The maximum amount of the interest rate on an adjustable rate mortgage can rise in a single year.

Rate of Depreciation:

Rate of depreciation gauges how fast your new purchase-automobile, computer, etc. will lose its market value.

Real Estate Secured Debt:

Any debt that has been used to buy a home or has been secured by your home. For example, a home equity loan can be a real estate secured debt.

Released:

A lien satisfied.

Renegotiable Rate Mortgage:

Periodic adjustment of an interest rate of a loan.

Report Number:

10 digit number that uniquely identifies each personal credit report.

Repossession:

When a creditor takes possession of property pledged as collateral on a loan to pay off the remaining loan amount.

Request an Investigation:

If you believe information on your credit report is inaccurate, you can request an investigation. Credit bureaus will ask the sources of the information to check their records at no cost to you. Incorrect information will be corrected; information that cannot be verified will be deleted. Accurate information cannot be removed from your credit report. An investigation may take up to 30 days. When it is complete, the credit bureau will send you the results, check these for accuracy immediately.

Request for Credit History

This is a request for your personal credit report. Consumer credit reports contain information a credit grantor can't see such as a detailed history of when your credit information is viewed by credit grantors or employers.

Reserve Officer Training Corps Scholarships (ROTC):

A program that exchanges money for college for services as a commissioned officer after graduation.

Residual Percent:

Remaining value of leased property at the end of the lease term, the higher the amount the lower your lease payment will be.

Right to Rescission:

By law the owner has three days to cancel a contract with respect to mortgage refinancing. Even after signing a contract, if the owner is using his home as equity in the title he has the legal right to void or cancel the mortgage contract. Right of Rescission is applicable to home equity loans.

Risk Based Pricing:

Fee structure used by creditors based on the risks of an individual.

Risk Levels:

To determine a credit score, lenders place you in a risk category that compares you to a large number of consumers with similar credit behavior.

Risk Score Models:
Used by credit grantors to predict future payment behavior of consumers. You can build in a hedge to this by limiting your applications for credit and your acceptance of pre approved cards.

Rolldown loan:
This is a loan whereas the lender pays all non-recurring closing costs for borrower. Borrower is still responsible for paying all pre-paid interest, property taxes, and hazard insurance as well as other recurring items. Minimum Rolldown loan is $150,000. Closing costs assume that borrower will escrow monthly property tax and insurance payments.

Sale or Deed:
Contract between purchaser and a seller of real estate to convey title after certain conditions have been met. It is a form of installment.

Sales Tax Rate:
Percentage of sales tax to be charged on a purchase. Sales tax for buying is charged on the total sales amount. In the case of a lease, sales tax is only due on the amount of the lease and is added to each lease payment.

Sallie Mae:
Corporate lender established to finance college for American families know as the Federal Family Education Loan Program (FFELP) under the Higher Education Act of 1965.

Satisfied:
If a consumer has paid all the money the court says he owes, the judgment is called "satisfied".

Scheduled Payment:
Payment due at a scheduled time. In the case of a home, the monthly principal and interest payment is based on your original mortgage amount, term and interest rate.

Score Factor:
Elements from a credit report that drive a credit score.

Secured Credit Card:
Credit card backed by a bank deposit account.

Security:
Real or personal property that a borrower pledges as collateral for the term of the loan. Should the borrower fail to repay, the creditor may take ownership of the secured property.

Security alert:
A statement added to one's Credit Report when a credit bureau is notified the consumer may be a victim of fraud. It remains on file 90 days. A Security Alert suggests that creditors should request proof of identification before granting credit in the person's name.

Security Interest:
The creditor's right to take property or a portion of property offered as security (collateral) for a loan.

Self Sufficiency Standards:
A measure of how much income is needed for families of a given composition, in a given place to adequately meet basic needs. The standard incorporates transportation and child care expenses for the working family. Regional and local variations in costs, family size and composition as well as the age of children determine the standard.

Seller's Points:
A lump sum paid by the seller to the buyer's creditor to reduce the cost of the loan to the buyer. This payment is either required by the creditor or volunteered by the seller, usually in a loan to buy a home.

Service Members Opportunity Colleges (SOC):
Consortium of 1500+ colleges and universities that provided educational assistance for servicemen and their families.

Settlement Costs:
All fees paid to the lender and mortgage broker, and certain other fees paid to third parties, which lenders do not control and for which they cannot provide accurate information until the origination process.

Settlement Date:
Date on which a statement is created, and the date used to calculate finance charges interest for the statement period.

Specific Bequest:
A particular item or specific dollar amounts to a specific individual or organization and a designated source for that bequest.

Stafford Loan:
The official name for student loans provided by private lenders and guaranteed against default by the government.

Statistical Models:
Statistical models are used to generate credit scores. Modelers analyze credit reports from millions of consumers to identify variables that determine future credit worthiness, i.e. credit score.

Student Loans:
Federal loans to finance education with very low interest rates. There are designations, student loans, parent loans, private loans and consolidated loans.

Student Loan Repayment Program:
Upon enlistment the Army will pay back up to $65,000 in qualified education loans (reservists qualify up to $20,000). The Navy pays up to $10,000. Alternative loans are not covered in this product.

Sub Prime:
Credit and loan products that have less stringent lending and loan approval terms and conditions with higher fees and rates to compensate for the higher risk.

Subsidized loans:
The government pays the interest to the lender while the borrower is in school.

Surcharge:
An extra fee for using a service. Surcharges are also referred to as convenience fees. This is a common practice with ATM machines.

Tax Savings:
Items that lower your taxable income. This includes the value of the tax deduction you receive by deducting interest payments for your mortgage.

Terms in Years:
Number of years to pay back a loan, most common mortgage terms are 15 and 30 years.

Thin file:
Credit report with few if any credit accounts or inquiry history.

Three C's:
Capacity, Collateral, and Credit. The primary areas used by creditors to measure your credit worthiness.

Title:
Written evidence proving right of ownership of a specific piece of property.

Title Insurance:
Protection both for lenders and homeowners against financial loss resulting from legal defects in the title.

Title Search:
An investigation into the history of ownership of a property to check for liens, unpaid claims, to prove the seller can transfer free and clear ownership.

Total Closing Costs:
Total up front costs paid before your loan can be issued. This is the sum of the loan origination fee, amount paid for points and any additional closing costs.

Total Debt Percent of Annual Income:
Percentage of annual income a financial institution will allow for use of installment debt. Installment debt includes car payments, credit card payment, other loan payments and your "Principal, Interest, Tax and Insurance (PITI) payment for your home.

Total debt Ratio:

Monthly debt and housing payment, divided by gross monthly income, to prove that the seller can transfer clear and free ownership.

Total down payment:

Amount available as a down payment, to be paid up front.

Total Interest:

Sum of interest paid.

Trade Line:

Each specific credit relationship with a business is tracked over time as a trade line on our credit report. You may have multiple accounts with the same bank, but your payment history will be identified separately for each account. Trade line information on your credit report includes company, date account was opened, credit limit, type of account, balance owed and payment profile.

Transaction Fees:

Fee charged for use of credit line, credit card, cash advances or ATM card.

Tuition Assistance (TA):

A military program allowing officers and enlisted service members to enroll at accredited colleges, universities and junior colleges.

Underwriting:

A process of evaluating a loan application to determine the risk involved for the lender that includes an analysis of the borrowers ability and willingness to pay.

Uniform Gift to Minors Act:

Custodial accounts for college planning that allows an adult custodian to manage the assets of a mutual fund or other investment account.

Uniform Transfer to Minors Act:
Custodial accounts for college planning that allows an adult custodian to manage the assets of a mutual fund or other investment account.

Usury:
Interest charged in excess of the legal rate established by law.

Unsecured credit:
Credit for which no collateral has been pledged.

Variable Rate:
Variable rate loans allow for an interest rate that fluctuates over the life of the loan. The rate is tied to an index reflecting changes in market rates of interest. A fluctuation in the rate causes changes in either the payments or the length of the loan term. Limits are often placed on the degree to which the interest rates can vary.

Verification:
With regard to credit reports, verification is the process of checking the accuracy of information. Credit grantors or employers may use your credit report information to verify application information.

Verification of Deposit:
Document signed by borrower's employer verifying his or her position and salary.

Warranty Deed:
The seller of real property warrants good title that is a guarantee that the current owner and previous owners have not impaired the title.

Will:
Formal document providing instructions on the disposition of property after death, setting out in detail each bequest and how property is to be disposed of. A will is created to decide who will be the guardian of your children as well as who will manage your estate.

Work Study Programs:
A federal program providing jobs for undergraduate and graduate students that need financial aid to attend college.

Writ of Replevin:
Legal document issued by a court authorizing repossession of property used to secure a loan

Wraparound Mortgage:
Results when an existing assumable loan is combined with a new loan, resulting in an interest rate somewhere between the old rate and the current market rate.

Appendix

More small print and other information to help you make the best choices as a consumer.

The Federal Fair Credit Reporting Act (FCRA) is designed to promote accuracy, fairness, and privacy of information in the files of every "consumer reporting agency" (CRA). Most CRAs are credit bureaus that gather and sell information about you – such as if you pay your bills on time or have filed bankruptcy – to creditors, employers, landlords, and other businesses. You can find the complete text of the FCRA 15 U.S.C. 1681-1681u, at the Federal Trade Commission's web site (http://www.ftc.gov). The FCRA gives you specific rights. You may have additional rights under state law. You may contact a state or local consumer protection agency or a state attorney general to learn those rights.

The FCRA gives several different federal agencies authority to enforce the act:

For questions or concerns regarding:	Please contact:
CRA's creditors, and others not listed below	Federal Trade Commission, Consumer Response Center Washington, DC 20580 202-326-3761
National banks, federal branches/agencies of foreign banks (word "National" or initials "N.A." appear in or after bank's name)	Office of the Comptroller of the Currency Compliance Management, Mail Stop 6-6 Washington, DC 20219 800-613-6743
Federal Reserve System member banks (except national banks, and federal branches/ agencies of foreign banks)	Federal Reserve Board, Division of Consumer & Community Affairs Washington, CD 20551 202-452-3693
Savings associations and federally chartered savings banks (word "Federal" or initials "F.S.B." appear in federal institution's name)	Office of Thrift Supervision, Consumer Programs Washington, DC 20552 800-842-6929
Federal credit unions (words "Federal Credit Union" appear in institution's name)	National Credit Union Administration, 1775 Duke Street Alexandria, VA 22314 703-518-6360

State chartered banks that are not members of the Federal Reserve System	Federal Deposit Insurance Corporation Division of Compliance & Consumer Affairs Washington, DC 20429 800-934-FDIC
Air, surface, or rail common carriers regulated by former Civil Aeronautics Board or Interstate Commerce Commission	Department of Transportation Office of Financial Management
Activities subject to the Packers and Stockyards Act, 1921	Department of Agriculture, Office of Deputy Administrator-GIPSA Washington, DC 20250 202-720-7051

Source: Federal Trade Commission

A Great Opportunity:

No Late Fees or Collection Calls!

Save with the highest rates in the nation!

Joe B. Anyone
1000 North Street
Anytown, USA

IıIıııIIıIIııııIııııIIıIIııIIıIIıııIıIıIıIIıııIIıI

Dear Joe B. Anyone

Now you can avoid potential late fees and collection calls by fully securing your ▮▮▮▮▮ Bank credit card account! If you secure your credit line with a matching security deposit, we will waive late fees and not telephone you for collection purposes if your payment is not made on time[1].

In addition to saving you money, we want to help you make money as well! A statement savings deposit with ▮▮▮▮▮ Bank is a great investment! With an Annual Percentage Yield of 3.04%[2], the ▮▮▮▮▮ Bank Statement Savings Account has one of the highest savings yields in the country[3]! In fact, our yields exceed the national average for statement savings accounts by 59%!

Start saving money – and making money – today! To open a statement savings account or make a deposit to your existing account, simply complete the form below, and enclose a check or money order for your deposit. To avoid future late fees and collection calls, your deposit must be at least $750. If you wish, deposit even more money into your statement savings account, and we will raise your credit line to match your deposit up to a maximum of $5,000!

Very truly yours,

Mary Sales

To open your savings account faster, visit us on the web at www.▮▮▮▮▮.com!

If you have questions about securing your account, please call 1-▮▮▮▮▮.

[1,2,3] See reverse for footnotes.

Statement Savings Account Opening Form

To open an account, just complete this form, detach, and return in the enclosed postage-paid envelope.
Do not send payments with this form. Any funds received in the enclosed envelope will be considered a deposit.

Please specify deposit amount: $ ☐.☐☐☐☐.☐☐   Minimum Deposit Required: $750

▮▮▮▮▮ Bank Credit Card Number

Social Security Number (TIN)
☐☐☐-☐☐-☐☐☐☐

( )   -
Home Phone Number - Required

( )   -
Work Phone Number - Required

TAX IDENTIFICATION NUMBER CERTIFICATION
Under penalty of perjury, you certify that (1) the number shown on this form is your correct Social Security Number and (2) you are not subject to backup withholding either because you have not been notified by the Internal Revenue Service (IRS) that you are subject to withholding as a result of a failure to report all interest and dividends, or that the IRS has notified you that you are no longer subject to backup withholding. *Cross out subpart (2) if you are subject to backup withholding.*

By submitting this form and depositing funds, I certify that I have read and agree to all of the terms, conditions, and disclosures in the footnotes and request that you open a ▮▮▮▮▮ Bank Statement Savings Account if I do not already have one, or deposit my funds into my existing Statement Savings Account.

Signature

CCCUB

[1]Late Fees may apply and you may receive collection calls if payments are past due on your credit account and charges or fees incurred cause your credit account balance to exceed its credit line (overlimit) or any portion of your credit line becomes unsecured. For example, a portion or all of your credit line may become unsecured if we allow a withdrawal from the deposit account or you obtain an unsecured credit line increase on your credit account. **Failure to make timely payments on your credit account will trigger the periodic rate for late payers as described in your agreement.** This offer may be discontinued at any time.

[2] **Statement Savings Account Information and Disclosures:** The interest rate on the Statement Savings Account ("Deposit") is 3.00% with an ANNUAL PERCENTAGE YIELD* ("APY") of 3.04%. The APY is accurate as of the date of this disclosure, however, the rate may change after the Deposit is opened, at our discretion. Interest will be compounded monthly and credited monthly. If you close your Deposit before interest is credited you will not receive the accrued interest. Interest is calculated using the average daily balance method, which applies a periodic rate to the average daily balance in the account for the period. Interest begins to accrue no later than the business day we receive credit for deposits made. There is no minimum balance required to open the Deposit and earn interest. Fees could reduce the earnings on the deposit. The Deposit will be owned jointly with the right to survivorship if more than one person applied for the Deposit and related credit card account. You will be sent Deposit statements not less than quarterly. We will promptly return your funds if a Deposit is not opened for any reason. **MEMBER FDIC**

Pledge And Assignment Of Statement Savings Account: By sending us money for deposit, you authorize ▇▇▇▇▇▇ Bank ▇▇▇▇ to open a Deposit to serve as collateral for your ▇▇▇▇ Credit Card Account ("Account"). Further, you hereby pledge and assign and grant ▇▇▇▇ a security interest in the Deposit and any sums you may later add to the Deposit to ▇▇▇▇, including interest you earn to secure payment of all obligations on the Account. This means your Deposit secures all sums you now or later owe us on your Account. You understand that the Deposit is subject to the Deposit agreement/rules and the Security section of the Account agreement and other documentation that will be sent to you. Further, you understand that the Deposit must remain with ▇▇▇▇ as long as it secures your Account, that ▇▇▇▇ need not permit any withdrawals from the Deposit and that if you fail to make any payments when they come due we may apply the Deposit to pay all that you owe on your Account without notice. This pledge and assignment shall be governed by Delaware Law.

*APY (Annual Percentage Yield) is the effective interest rate your money will earn if it remains on deposit for a full year at the same annual interest rate, and if all of the principal and interest are left in the account.

[3] Source: ▇▇▇▇▇▇▇▇▇▇ April 1, 2002. Rate comparisons are for Money Market accounts.

P.O. BOX 5098 / SIOUX FALLS, SD 57117-5098

Congratulations! You're **PRE-APPROVED** for a New   Card.

Pre-Approved Account For:

Joe P. Anyone
1000 North Ave
Any Town USA

|||ıı||ıı||ıı||ıı||ıı||ıı||ıı||ıı||ıı||ı|||ı|

MAXIMUM
CREDIT LIMIT UP TO:
$1,500.00*
RESPOND BY:

July 5, 2002

Dear Joe P. Anyone

Your good standing has been found creditworthy by ▨▨▨▨ and that qualifies you for a new ▨▨▨ account. No security deposit and no savings account are required for you to accept this card. (See insert for details.)

Grace period for repayment of balances for purchases	If you pay the previous balance in full on or before the due date shown on the previous statement, you will have a grace period on purchases of 25 days (from the statement closing date to the payment due date) and can avoid finance charges on current purchases by paying the current statement in full on or before the payment due date.
Method of computing the balances for purchases	Average Daily Balance (Including new purchases)
Annual Fees	Annual Membership Fee: $50; Participation Fee: $72 annually ($6 monthly); Optional Additional Card Fee: $20 annually
Minimum FINANCE CHARGE	$0.50
Transaction fee for cash advances	Greater of $5 or 3% of the amount of the cash advance
Fees for issuance or availability of credit	Processing Fee: $29 (One-Time Only); Acceptance Fee: $119 (One-Time Only); First Credit Limit Increase Fee: $25 (One-Time Only) Optional Express Mail Card: $25; Optional Automatic Payment: $5; Express Processing Fee: $6 (Optional & One-Time Only)
Fees for paying late, exceeding credit limit	Late Fee: $20 each time payment is late; Over Limit Fee: $20 each month the balance exceeds the credit limit
Annual Percentage Rate	18.9%

Fees for other services: Copying Charge: $5 per document; Returned Payment Fee: $20 for each payment returned from your bank.

Guidelines and sample clauses for wills.

It is not an expensive process to have an attorney draft a will for you. However, you may keep billable hours at a bare minimum if you start the process. Your attorney will take your draft and write the will according to the contingencies and special considerations regarding the legality of a last will and testament in your state.

If you are considering a handwritten will the provisions and signature must be in the handwriting of the person making the will. Most states do not accept holographic wills. Each state that does has different regulations regarding an executor and bonds. Unless you find yourself in a life-threatening situation and you do not have a will, it is advised to have your will professionally prepared and typewritten.

Check list:
- Full name of the testator(s)
- Executor
- Full names of the beneficiaries
- Estate Value and identification
-   • Bequests specific and general
- Did you date the will?
- Did you identify yourself in the will by giving your full name and address?
- Did you identity this document as your last will and testament?
- Did you clearly dispose of all your property through provisions of the will?
- Are the bequests detailed enough to be understood clearly?
- Did you sign and date your signature at the end of the will?
- If you are writing a joint will, are all the provisions for a joint will clearly stated?
- Did you set up a guardianship for your children?
- Did you name the individual that will manage your estate?
- Did you number the pages of the will?
- Did you have the will witnessed and notarized? (This is if you are not seeking the services of an attorney.)
- Did you place your will in a safe place where your executor and survivors can find it?
- Did you make more than one copy of your will?

Be Sure you date your will!

Sample clauses:

I, Frances Anne Hernan, of Johnson County, Kansas, being of sound mind and under no undue influence, make my last will and testament, revoking all previous wills and codicils.

Furthermore, I direct that all my just debt be paid as soon after my death as possible. I direct that any monies left from my funeral insurance go to covering expenses of administering my estate.

I appoint my brother, John Doe as my personal representative, to serve without bond. If he is unable to serve, I appoint Joseph Smith as my personal representative, also to serve without bond.

I wish to have my personal and household effects distributed as follows:

(List each item and the individual or organization the property is being left to.) **For example:** Baseball Card Collection to the Boys and Girls Club of Olathe, Kansas

I give the residue of my estate, real and personal to my spouse, (full name) if she/he survives me. In the event my spouse does not survive me, I give the residue of my estate to my children, to be divided equally (name exceptions) . If one of my children fails to survive me, his/her shares shall be divided equally among his/her children OR his/her shares shall be divided among my surviving children.

I give the residue of my estate, real and personal, as follows:
- 50 % to my surviving spouse
- 25% to my daughter
- 25% to my brother John Doe

Optional clauses and declarations:

I declare that I am married to (full name) and intend to confirm to my spouse his/her half of our community property and to dispose of my half of our community property and all of my separate property.

I give to my church (name and location) the sum of $
_____.

I give to my nephew, Justin Jones the sum of $
_____ if he survives me.

If you are married for a second time and you intend to leave the bulk of your estate to your surviving children and not your spouse include a provision that ensures your children will inherit all of your estate that you intend for them.

I declare that both my spouse (name) and I have our own property and that I will if he/ she should predeceases me, claim no homestead exemption, exempt property, or family allowances from his/her estate; and I hereby direct that my spouse (name) receive no homestead allowances, exempt property, or family allowances from my estate.

INSURANCE

It is important to determine what you need in terms of life insurance before you come face to face with an insurance salesman. Remember they are working on commission. This checklist will help you calculate how much insurance you need.

How much annual income will your family need?

List the amount you would like to provide for your beneficiaries each year for the number of years until your youngest child is 18/21. When estimating this amount consider college expenses, health care expenses and childcare expenses.
- How much interest do you expect your beneficiaries to receive on your residuary?
- Estimate the annual rate of return to coincide with the above amount that you which to provide until based on your income projections until your child/children reach the age of 18/21.
- Estimate the annual inflation rate you expect to offset a portion of the interest projecting the next 20 years based on the history of the past ten years.
- Determine the value of your home. Enter the current value, this number is used to offset your net worth.
- List all outstanding debt. Estimate the interest on the debt that will need to be paid off.
- Estimate the total value for your estate. Include the equity you have in your home but do not deduct the loans/debt payments included above.
- List existing life insurance and plan new insurance to update your coverage and fill in the gaps.

LIVING WILLS

A living will protects you when you cannot speak for yourself.

A living will often referred to as The Will To Live (National Right to Life) protects you when you cannot speak for yourself in the event you develop a condition that makes it impossible for you to speak for yourself . The living will makes clear through written instructions to your health care agent what medical treatment you would want when you cannot speak for yourself.

The living will should be created in the following way:

- Name a person you trust to safeguard your life when you cannot speak for yourself as your "health care agent".
- Name a backup agent(s) when your first choice can't serve.
- Describe the treatment you do and do not want to guide your health care agent and physicians (use of life support systems etc.).

Your living will protects your family and health care agents from pressure from health care providers and others by allowing them to prove what you really want. A living will also relieves the agony of decision making by carrying out your wishes regarding your health care in the even you become incompetent.

Index

Accelerated payment-83
Acceleration clause-83
Acceptance-83
Account condition-83
Account monitoring-83
Adverse Action Notice-28,29,83,84
Adjustable rate mortgage-83
Adjusted basis-84
Adjustment Interval-84
Affordability analysis-84
Aid package-85
Amortization-85
Annual Fee-85
Annual income-85
Annual Percentage Rate- 54,56
Annual rate of return-86
Appraisal-86
Association code-86
Assumption-86
Bankruptcy code-64,87
Big Three-88
Billing cycle-50,88
Budget-,15,16,17,18,88,
Campus based aid-89
Caps (Interest)-89
Capacity-89
Cash advances-35
Certificate of Title-89
Certificate of Veteran Status-89
Closing costs and Closing-89
Collateral-89

Combined Loan to Value-56
Consolidation loan-90
Consumer Credit Counseling Service-90
Consumer credit information-90
Convenience checks-45
Coverdell Education Saving Accounts-
Credit file-,26,27,32,33,35,36
Credit History-33,35,91
Credit investigation-32,33,91
Credit report-25,26,27,30,32,33
Credit Reporting Agencies-24,26,28,30,31,35,36,37,49
Credit Scores-25,27,28,92
Debt to income ratio-92
Debt management-63,67
Discount Points-93
Education IRA-79
Effective interest rate-94
Equifax-33
Fair Credit and Charge Disclosure Act-95
Fair Credit Billing Act (FCBA)-94
The Fair Credit Reporting Act (FCRA)-23,30
Federal Family Loan Education Program-68
Federal Trade Commission-23,30,35,50,52,63,82
Federal Housing Administration (FHA)-96
FICO Score-96
Flood Insurance-96
Forbearance-73,96
Foreclosure-97
High Risk-28,97
Home equity loan-56,57
Home equity closing costs-97
Home equity interest rate-98
Home equity line of credit-57,
Identity theft-49,50,98
Impound-98
Interest rate-55
Inquiry-98
Investigative consumer reports-99
Line of credit- 100
Loan origination rate-100
Loan to value ratio-100

Medical Information Bureau-
MIP Mortgage Insurance Premium-
Montgomery GI Bill-101
Negative amortization-101
Notice of results-
Opt out-51,52,110
Pay day loan-47,48,102
PELL grant-73,102
Permissible purposes-103
Private Mortgage Insurance PMI-104
Pre-approved credit card-39,40,41,42,43
Public record data-31,32
Rate of depreciation-105
Rate cap-105
Real estate secured debt-105
Report number-105
Repossession-105
Request an investigation-105
Right to rescission-59
Risk score models-25,106
Sallie Mae-68
Security alert-108
Stafford Loan-72,109
Statistical models-109
Student Loans-67
Student Loan Repayment Program-67
Tax savings-110
Title-110
Title Insurance-110
Title Search-110
Total closing costs-110
Total debt percent of annual income-110
Total debt Ratio-111
Truth in Lending Act-58,
Tuition Assistance-111
Uniform Gift to Minors Act-77
Uniform Transfer to Minors Act-77
Variable rate-112
Verification-112
Verification of deposit-112
Wraparound mortgage-112